UNBINDING
your
SOUL

The Unbinding the Gospel Series
by Martha Grace Reese

In more than 12,000 congregations in 50 states, 49 denominations, 8 countries...

"Evangelism" is anything you do to help someone move closer to a relationship with God, or into Christian community

What's Your Church's Question? *WHY, or HOW?*

Evangelism books presume everyone wants to do evangelism, so they tell you *how* to do it. Six years of national, Lilly Endowment-funded research in nine denominations have demonstrated conclusively that most people would rather get a root canal than think about evangelism. You can tell people to "go be missional" until the cows come home. They just won't do it until they *want* to.

If we answer the "WHY share my faith? question, we'll start wanting to know "HOW can God use me to help people move into faith?" Our churches can't share their faith until they're loving, relational communities where people (1) pray, and (2) talk comfortably with each other about their own faith experiences. Once our churches make this shift, we'll want to know *HOW* to share our faith. The *Unbinding the Gospel Series* addresses both the *Why* and the *How.*

Take a Quiz. Decide where *your* church should start. Think about your congregation. Check all statements that apply:

- ❏ *You* do evangelism! I'm going to alphabetize the Sunday School closet.
- ❏ Evangelism's why I left my old church. I don't want to embarrass friends.
- ❏ Nobody's going to make *me* pass out tracts.
- ❏ Evangelism is theologically inappropriate. It's not our ethos.
- ❏ Whoa! God's doing exciting things in my life and through our church! How can I help my friends connect with this?

WHY churches check boxes 1-4. *HOW* churches check only box 5. So, are you a *WHY* church, or a *HOW* church? [Martha Grace Reese, author of the Series and director of the Mainline Evangelism Project and the Unbinding the Gospel Project (the Lilly studies), estimates that 90% of U.S. churches are *WHY* churches!]

WHY churches can become *HOW* churches if they start with *Unbinding the Gospel,* then do an all-church saturation study with *Unbinding Your Heart. HOW* churches can move into joyful faith sharing with *Unbinding Your Soul.*

"WHY" Churches START with *GOSPEL/HEART*

STEP ONE— Church Leaders' Study: *Unbinding the GOSPEL (red ribbon).* Start with a "test" small group study with leaders who you think will like it best. Optimal group size: 8-10 members, pastor leads. (DON'T preach or write newsletter articles – you'll only create resistance! Remember: In people's heads, "Evangelism" = "Root Canal".) Pastor: read the introduction and chapters 1 & 4 of *Unbinding Your Church* and skim *Unbinding Your Soul* now. They will help you lead your *GOSPEL* studies effectively.

- **Study GOSPEL** in small groups over eight weekly sessions
- **Do the exercises** at the ends of the chapters
- **Pray** with 40-day prayer journal after discussing chapter 3

If **Gospel** helps, keep going! Move on to more small-group studies of **GOSPEL** with your church leaders and teachers (20% of your worship attendance).

red ribbon

STEP TWO—All-Church Saturation Study: *Unbinding Your Heart (purple ribbon)* is a six-week version of **Unbinding the Gospel** with a different individual prayer journal. We see significant changes in churches that bring the "unbinding" experience to at least 85% of worship attendance. Each week, for 40 days, people will:

purple ribbon

- **Pray** each day's scripture and prayer exercise & work with a prayer partner
- **Study** a chapter with their small group
- **Worship** – sermon, music & prayers centered on the week's chapter

SUPPORT FOR STEPS ONE & TWO— Pastor's and Leaders' Guide: *Unbinding Your Church (green ribbon). **Unbinding Your Church** offers "best practices" for small group leaders, prayer teams, youth leaders, pastors. It provides comprehensive organizational aids, coordinated resources for children and youth, worship, full music plans in four styles & 7 sample sermons.

green ribbon

"HOW" Churches Use *SOUL*

Unbinding Your Soul: Your Experiment in Prayer & Community (yellow ribbon) is for:

- *Churches that have finished their E-vents*
- *New churches*
- *New members' classes*
- *Young adult / college groups*

Soul is where churches reach out! Many people who aren't connected with a church would love to try a no-obligation experience of substantial spiritual discussion, prayer and community. **Unbinding Your Soul** prepares church members to invite their friends into a 4-week small group experience with short study chapters, an individual prayer journal, prayer partner activities & group exercises. **Includes facilitators' & pastors' guides, plus sermons & resources for an all-church experience!**

yellow ribbon

Thinking of using the Series? Review all four books at the beginning. **Unbinding Your Soul** will help **WHY** churches see a trajectory toward becoming a **HOW** church. **SOUL** is laced with 70 stories and direct quotes from a huge range of churches that have worked with the **Series**. See **www.GraceNet.info** for info, videos & resources.

To Grandmother and Grandad

Martha Grace Miller Reese

and

Everett David Reese

UNBINDING *your* SOUL

Your Experiment in Prayer & Community

Small Group Studies & Personal Prayer Journal

Martha Grace Reese

CHALICE
PRESS

ST. LOUIS, MISSOURI

Cover photograph: GettyImages
Photograph of author: David Bjerk
Cover and interior design: Elizabeth Wright

Visit Chalice Press on the World Wide Web at
www.chalicepress.com

10 9 8 7 6 5 4 3 2   10   11   12   13   14   15

EPUB: 978-0-8272-38169   EPDF: 978-0-8272-38176

Library of Congress Cataloging–in–Publication Data

Reese, Martha Grace.
    Unbinding your soul : your experiment in prayer & community / by Martha Grace Reese.
        p. cm. — (Unbinding the gospel series)
    "Small group, study & prayer journal."
    ISBN 978-0-8272-3809-1
    1. Prayer—Christianity—Textbooks. 2. Small groups—Religious aspects—Christianity. I. Title. II. Series.

    BV215.R44 2009
    248.3'2—dc22

                                                        2009026754

Printed in the United States of America

Contents

Acknowledgments

Unbinding Your Soul arises out of the efforts, stories and generosity of thousands of people. Research underlying *Unbinding the Gospel*, the cornerstone book of the *Unbinding Series*, involved hundreds of congregations across the country, as well as 1200 personal interviews. Thank you to each of you, many of whom I've only "met" on the phone. Your voices still resonate in me. Your accumulated wisdom has helped tens of thousands of people and churches across the country.

Many of the people who have used *Unbinding the Gospel* and *Unbinding Your Heart* over the last three years have reflected on their and their churches' experiences with the process. You've taught us much. Your learnings, your words and your stories undergird *Unbinding Your Soul.* Thank you to those who have called me, sent me e-mails, and particularly those who have been part of the new *Unbinding the Gospel Project.* You have reflected, written answers to questions and collected statistics for us. I suspect that all your effort, some of which is reflected in this book, will help many people. Thank you!!!

I've worked with about 100 large groups of pastors and lay leaders in person over the last two years. It was terrific to see you in person and to hear your thoughts and reactions. You've taught me so much. You've shaped this book.

The Religion Division of the Lilly Endowment, Inc. has helped make the *Unbinding* work a reality. They have awarded two grants to fund this research, the *Mainline Evangelism Project (2002-2007)* and the *Unbinding the Gospel Project (2008-).* The Endowment's support of the church in this country adds to all our lives. Thank you, particularly, to Craig Dykstra and Chris Coble. I'm so grateful for your help, wisdom and encouragement. Chris, I owe you, and probably the rest of the Endowment staff, for the chapter 3 title. Thank you!

Thank you also to the heads of denominations and key national church leaders who helped the Mainline Evangelism Project get started, supported it through the research phase, helped launch *Unbinding the Gospel*: Jim Griffith, Dick Hamm, George Hunter, Todd Hunter, Cliff Kirkpatrick, Brian McLaren, Roy Medley, Stan Noffsinger, Richard Peace, John Thomas and Sharon Watkins.

The *Unbinding the Gospel Project* exists for two reasons: (1) to help 1000 congregations begin to pray, develop deeper faith and to share that faith by working by means of the *Unbinding Series*; and (2) to gather stories and data from those churches so that we can help more churches start moving. The Project rests on a team.

First and foremost is Elinor ("Ellie") Campbell, our Project Administrator. Her spirit, graciousness, and spiritual, literary, and organizational gifts underpin all we're doing. If we meet our grant's goal, it will be because diminutive Ellie Campbell is carrying us all on her shoulders, like Hercules and the World. Thank you, Ellie, from all who are blessed to work with you.

Thank you, wonderful coaches, who have given so much time, thought and skill to developing our coaching model and serving your churches: Pamela Dolan, Nancy Lee Gauche, Jeff Gill, Paul Nickerson, Cathy Townley, and Nancy Wood. Your creativity, insight, skill and persistence as we've developed this model inspire me. It's an honor and just plain fun to work together. Thank you so much.

I'm particularly grateful to Nancy Lee Gauche, our coaching director. Her wonderful systemic sense and gentle guidance of the coaching process bless us all. Thank you, NLG! Judy Hall and PJ Patterson—thank you for your kind, patient, gracious and efficient bookkeeping help.

Dave Yankowiak is our brilliant web guy. The visible parts of *www.GraceNet.info* are but the tip of the iceberg. Hidden in the depths are data collection, information dissemination and coaching support systems that would awe NASA. We are utterly cool.

Dear friends and colleagues have read this manuscript in various stages. Thank you, each of you, for your sage advice, suggestions and fabulous kindness! Ann Azdell, Ellen McNeary Briggs, Liz Bowman, Ellie Campbell, Hilary Chittick, Laura Durfey Cuaz, Anne DeFuria, Andrea Hammerschmidt Felkins, MJ Fitch, Nancy Lee Gauche, Jeff Gill, Elizabeth Harman, Steve Hayner, Ray Jones, Tryna Loos, Nikki MacMillan, Helen Haskell McCallum, Gil Reese, Jim Riley, Don Schutt, Jackie Solem, Viv Jones Stretten, Cathy Townley, Sharon Tutko, Russ White and Sarah White.

Roger Ross, it has been a privilege to partner with you over the last year. Thank you for the beautiful account of First United Methodist's *Unbinding* work, at page 156.

Don Schutt, our years as prayer partners serve as an underlayment to my work and my life—thank you.

Chalice Press has been gracious and skillful throughout the three years we've worked together on the ***Unbinding Series***. I'm so grateful to each of you for everything you've done to make these books a reality. Wes Buchek, Trent Butler, Bill Breeden, John Carey, Rob Hudson, Lynne Letchworth, Cindy Meilink, Amber Moore, Lisa Scronce, Gail Stobaugh, Connie Wang, Russ White and Elizabeth Wright—you all are wonderful!

Finally, to my family—I've used a lot of fabulous Reese stories. I'm so grateful to you all for a lifetime of love, support, challenges, learning and opportunities. And thank you, beloved nuclear family—Russ, Elizabeth and Sarah. You girls are such great sports—Sarah burst out laughing and Elizabeth, with her literary eagle eye, actually sharpened the caricature of the Girls in the Woods story that opens chapter 2. I love you guys so much!

Russ White—prayer partner, dearest friend, beloved husband—none of this would be possible without you, for so many reasons. Really.

MGR
Marcell, Minnesota

Introduction

How to Use This Book

I've spent the last 15 years leading national research projects focused on faith, spirituality, and the transformation and growth of Christian communities. I've spoken in depth/interviewed over two thousand people during this time. Some of them have no connection with organized religion. Many more are Christians—pastors, church leaders, and new and long-time Christians across the country.[1]

I hear one message clearly: ***Most people want real friends.*** Most people want to be able to talk honestly about their lives and about significant life issues. Most people have some kind of a spiritual life. Millions of people in and out of churches would love to try an authentic test of a faith community—a confidential, loving, hopeful, real group of people. They'd like to explore, to think about, to talk with other people about God, about Jesus, about what's possible in a human life. Loads of people would like to work with some ancient prayer practices. Christian prayer and community are extraordinary and can be life changing.

I hear something else: ***No one wants to be trapped.*** We wouldn't buy a car sight unseen. We'd test-drive it. Loads of people who don't go to church would love to try a short, non-obligating, "test-drive" of Christianity—as long as they didn't get stuck. They'd like something short term, intense, and not watered down. A lot of Christians feel the same way. They'd like to try something more "real," more substantial than just dropping by church most Sundays—as long as it wasn't weird, or they didn't commit themselves for too long. So loads of people want the same thing— to try an experiment in a substantial type of faith and spirituality, to talk about what's really going on in their lives.

The predicament: Hideous cartoons of evangelism lurk in our heads. I've led the only major, national study of evangelism in the seven specific denominations called "Mainline Churches." I can tell you for a fact, after four years of intensive research, that people who don't go to church cringe at the idea of strangers harassing them with humiliating, condescending questions about whether they're saved. But that's ***nothing*** compared to the horror with which members of churches hear the word "evangelism." The word hits the eardrum. Christians break out in a cold sweat and start lacing on their Adidas.[TM]

Recap: Most people want to have friends they can trust. They want to talk about significant life and faith issues and to try some classic Christian prayer disciplines. But ***no one*** wants to sound like a honey-crusted nut bar.[2] No one wants to be stuck in a room with a bunch of loonies. No one wants to embarrass a friend.

A Solution: Unbinding Your Soul can provide the foundation for a four-week "test-drive" of Christian friendship, discussion, community, and classic prayer disciplines. I'm going to call it "Your Experiment in Prayer & Community." Use it as a test. See if you like it. Give it your best efforts for four weeks. At the end of the four weeks, you're done. No one will bug you. No one will expect you to stay. After four meetings and three weeks of working with different types of prayer, you'll have a good idea whether this is any kind of fit for you. *"The Experiment" is Part One of this book. When you want to go deeper, Part Two, "Faith & Courage" is waiting for you!*

Church People—I know this is hard. People have told you not to be pushy or rude your whole Christian life. (Or they may **have** told you to be pushy and rude, but you've cowered in corners or wanted to come out swinging.) One way or the other, Christians all over the country are walking around, quietly traumatized by horrific visions of arguing people into bumper sticker truth and forcing pamphlets into the hands of frantically reluctant strangers. Unfortunately, those bad cartoons have stopped many of us from mentioning to our best friends that we love the church we're part of, and that our faith is the core of our lives. I think that's problematic. We don't have to be **quite** such timid woodland creatures. So here's the deal:

1. You don't have to do anything embarrassing.

2. Try *The Experiment* yourselves, in a small group from your church. If you like it, do Part Two, *Faith & Courage*. If you decide to keep going, you can each invite someone who doesn't normally go to church to do Part I, *The Experiment,* with you. Who's a real friend? Who has an interesting life and fascinating ideas on other subjects? With whom do you want to spend some significant time? With whom would **you** like to talk about faith issues and about **your** life? *That's* the person you invite into *The Experiment.* You can invite your whole golf foursome or your string quartet if you want.

3. If you like it, keep going and do *Faith & Courage*. Anyone who wants to keep going (the friends you invited, perhaps), can invite more people into *The Experiment*. But keep going in 4-week commitments - no one is obligated for more than 4 weeks!

A Level Playing Field: Friends of these Christians—if you're invited into *The Experiment,* thanks for considering being part of it. You may have had some horrible experience of someone haranguing you with biblical proof-texts or humiliating questions. This group isn't about that. You're not the guinea pig. It's YOUR experiment!

The purpose of this group is to create a fun, safe place for everyone to have significant conversations. The purpose of the group is to think a bit about some big questions—Is there a God? How can I know? How do you pray? What's true about the world? How can we live together best? How should I spend my life? How can I walk with God, every day, learning and not clotting? The purpose of the group is to talk about what **you** want to talk about! What's happening in your life? It will be a new experience for everyone—people who go to church each week, people who don't. This is a level playing field.

No one is selling anything. No one will try to convert or manipulate you.

However, I can't imagine a group of eight or ten people not changing a little if they talk honestly for four meetings, and pray in between. Let me be as honest as I can be about my presuppositions and worldview: I'm a Christian, I believe that God exists, loves us, and wants us to become much more spiritually aware, more hopeful, more deeply connected with other people, more joy-filled, more committed to living a life that's rich with serving other people. (I also believe all that's possible!)

My hope for the outcome of this month together is that you'll get to know each other better and that you will take whatever "next steps" God would like you to take. God can, and will, do amazing things *in our lives* and ***through us*** if we'll just pay attention and follow.

This is a pretty humble process. It isn't rocket science. It's spiritual growth. We trust that God will bless our lives and take us to the next deeper level if we'll talk honestly with each other, listen carefully and respectfully to each other, study bits of the Bible and pray. Four weeks isn't very long, so let's not tiptoe around the main point or fuss around with leading up to it gently. You all are interested enough to agree to meet four times and to pray for three weeks. Let's get started!

> See video from an Experiment Group:
> *www.GraceNet.info/video.aspx*
> 1st Presbyterian Church, Gainesville, FL
> If you're not in college, it will make you want to go!

---

[1] The *Mainline Evangelism Project* was a major, four-year study of highly effective evangelism in seven denominations, made possible by a grant from the Lilly Endowment (Martha Grace Reese, Project Director). Congregations studied were affiliated with the American Baptist Churches, USA, Christian Church (Disciples of Christ), Evangelical Lutheran Church in America, Presbyterian Church USA, Reformed Church in America, United Church of Christ and The United Methodist Church. See *Unbinding the Gospel,* 2nd ed. by Martha Grace Reese (Chalice Press, 2008), the cornerstone book of the *Unbinding the Gospel Series.* The first two pages of this book describe the Series. More information is available at the very end of this book, at *Next Steps.* Look at *www.GraceNet.info* for general information on the Lilly Endowment-funded grants, the purposes of the studies and the current *Unbinding the Gospel Project* grant. A full Wenger-Reese sociological report detailing the statistical results of the *Mainline Evangelism Project* is available at www.GraceNet.info / Download Resources.

[2] Aaron Sorkin, *Studio 60 on the Sunset Strip,* 2007.

Research Basis of *Unbinding Your Soul*

Quotes & Stories Cited

Unbinding Your Soul arises from, reflects findings of, and projects courses of action premised upon two national research projects, both funded by the Lilly Endowment, Inc. and directed by Martha Grace Reese: the *Mainline Evangelism Project* (2002-2007) and the *Unbinding the Gospel Project* (2008-). Primary findings of *the Mainline Evangelism Project* may be found in ***Unbinding the Gospel, 2nd ed.*** (Reese, Chalice Press, 2008), as well as in a sociological report on the primary quantitative data of the Mainline Evangelism Research Project by Jacqueline E. Wenger, Ph.D of Catholic University and Martha Grace Reese, J.D., M.Div. (download from *www.GraceNet.info / Download Resources / Public Downloads*).

Unbinding Your Soul is laced with about 70 stories and direct quotes arising from the first 18 months of the second research grant, the *Unbinding the Gospel Project*. This newest research has influenced the scope, character and trajectory of this book. In simplest terms, ***Unbinding Your Soul*** should help typical congregations move fluidly and organically into the transformative shifts that arise spontaneously with the Spirit in "quick adapter" congregations using the ***Unbinding the Gospel/Heart*** process most effectively. In SAT terms, Jim Collins'

> ***Built to Last***[1] is to ***Unbinding the Gospel*** as
> ***Good to Great***[2] is to ***Unbinding Your Soul***

The stories and quotations in ***Unbinding Your Soul*** come from persons involved with the *Unbinding the Gospel Project*. The purpose of the grant is to provide both coaching for 1000 congregations and ongoing research on congregational transformation and faith sharing. Groups of congregations formally admitted into the grant process work through an all-church saturation study of ***Unbinding the Gospel*** and ***Unbinding Your Heart,*** then move on to small group use of ***Unbinding Your Soul.*** (See "Next Steps," page 151 and *www.GraceNet.info* for more information.)

Stories and quotations used in this book (within the context of chapters, as sidebar quotations, as foundations for author statements, and in stand-alone quotes at the beginnings of chapters), unless otherwise attributed, come from interviews, reports or written statements by people connected with the *Unbinding the Gospel Project*. Unattributed sidebar quotes in quotation marks are from participants in the *Unbinding the Gospel Project*. Sidebar quotes without quotation marks are by Martha Grace Reese.

In accordance with our agreement with participants, all contributed writings and stories are used without attribution, and with details disguised for purposes of confidentiality. A few of the most typical quotes are composites. Full names, denominational indicators, and physical locations of churches, where given, are accurate and used with permission. Use of a first name alone is pseudonynomic. Some quotations have been edited for brevity and clarity.

Thank you to each of you who has talked with us or written one of these powerful, personal reflections. You are in our prayers. You inspire us, and we're pretty sure you're going to inspire others. Keep those cards and letters coming!

---

[1]Jim Collins and Jerry I. Porras, *Built to Last: Successful Habits of Visionary Companies* (New York: HarperBusiness Essentials, 2002).

[2]Jim Collins, *Good to Great: Why Some Companies Make the Leap… and Others Don't* (New York: CollinsBusiness, 2001).

Prepare for First Meeting— Part One Reading Assignment

Read Introduction, chapter 1 and <u>Using Your Prayer Journal</u> (pages xi–10 & 123–131) <u>before</u> your first group meeting.

Start Week A of your Prayer Journal the day <u>after</u> your first group meeting.

The gray-tipped pages are for you!

Unbinding Your Soul

PART ONE | The Experiment

*Four Weeks of Prayer
& Community*

■ **PART ONE**
    The Experiment in Prayer & Community

■ **PART TWO**
    Faith & Courage

■ **PART THREE**
    Resources to Help with the Unbinding

    • Using Your Prayer Journal
    • Facilitators' & Pastors' Guides
    • Next Steps

*...those who wait for the LORD shall renew their strength,
they shall mount up with wings like eagles,
they shall run and not be weary,
they shall walk and not faint.
(Isaiah 40:31)*

Life turns on a dime…

The Oxford Project is a study in photos and stories of people in Oxford, Iowa (pop. 676). Peter Feldstein took photographic portraits of almost everyone in town in 1984. Twenty years later, he went back to Oxford with his camera, and with Stephen Bloom, a writer. The book astounds with powerful images and stories of people's lives. Why would small town Iowans talk so openly with two East Coast strangers? One woman responded:

"He said, 'Tell me about your life.' How often does somebody ask you that: Tell me about your life?"

"I walked away from this knowing that life turns on a dime," Bloom said. "I realized that life is really dependent on moments, and you don't know when those moments are going to take place when you wake up. And sometimes when you go to sleep at night, you don't realize those moments have taken place."[1]

CHAPTER 1

Get Started

I grew up in central Ohio. Pretty much everyone went to church. The church we ***didn't*** attend was Presbyterian. We didn't go on Christmas. We didn't go on Easter. My grandparents lived next door. Grandad went to church every Sunday. He was a banker, a philanthropist who helped thousands of people during the course of his life, and a Welsh Presbyterian. My Grandmother also made everybody's life way more wonderful, but she did ***not*** go to church.

Grandmother was fascinating! She could simultaneously knit with two strands of yarn, jingle her gold grandmother's charm bracelet, keep an eye on the roast and the potatoes in the oven, flip her shoe on the end of her foot, and read *Little Lord Fauntleroy*[2] out loud to me for the fourteenth time. We loved Grandmother. I was the oldest and got to be named Martha Grace Reese after her. She taught me everything—how to knit, to bake bread, and to recite the kings and queens of England from Ethelred the Unready to Elizabeth II.

Grandmother said that religion was for people who didn't have Other Resources. She demonstrated, with vivid examples, how leaders had used simple people's faith to manipulate them into wars and into submission. She stressed (bracelet clanking as she knit a snowsuit for someone's daughter's second twin) that every army that had marched through Europe since Genghis Khan had carried the banner of Jesus in the vanguard of the battle. "Well-educated people," she articulated, knitting needles clicking furiously, "should ***know*** about religion, but no one who has the sense God gave a ***goat*** would believe it." That was my beloved, sainted grandmother! We adored her.

3

I emerged from my childhood with a firm grasp on history, literature, music, knitting, the kings and queens of England, how to turn cables in a sweater, and when to flip the potatoes under the roast. A *couple* of gaps remained. Like, for instance, I thought *Amazing Grace* was a Judy Collins song.

I spent my junior year in college at the University of Madrid. I met Hilary, who was

a. a Christian

b. smart (she's a judge now), and

c. talked about Jesus as if there actually *were* one!

It was a whole new world. I hadn't known that there were smart Christians. I know *now* that I knew lots of Christians, many of whom were very bright. Some of them probably had significant spiritual lives. They just never talked about them to me.

Heavens, my **Grandad** was a brilliant man, immensely articulate, and a devoted Christian. I learned as an adult that his faith motivated a huge amount of his service to people. He and I took hundreds of long walks over the years, just the two of us. We talked about people, business, banking, education, community development, service to people, racism, other countries, international relations, doing things that matter with your life, *but he never mentioned his faith.*

I thought Grandad helped revitalize redlined neighborhoods, raised money for Ohio State, worked so hard with developing nations' national banking systems, and was one of the most amazing people on earth because he was **Welsh**. I didn't realize that a lot of it also could have been because he was a Welsh **Presbyterian**. How many of his firmly held, innovative, and courageous ideas were forged in his deeply private, religious convictions? I don't know. As far as I knew, he never talked about church, faith or God. Grandmother had all the airspace on the subject.

But Hilary, in Spain, talked with me about what she believed and what she had experienced as a Christian. I read Spanish religious writers in class at school. I read existentialists too long and late at night. Hilary and I talked about what I thought and about what she believed. I was thrown for a loop to consider all these intangible, invisible possibilities for the way the world might be.

After a particularly intense talk one day on the way home from school, she handed me her Bible, with slips of paper marking two spots: Ecclesiastes and the Gospel of John. Then she left. Ecclesiastes

---

Most people want to have friends they can trust. They want to talk about significant life and faith issues and to try some classic Christian prayer disciplines. But *no one* wants to sound like a honey-crusted nut bar. No one wants to be stuck in a room with a bunch of loonies. No one wants to embarrass a friend.

and John toppled me into a powerful conversion experience. I realized over the course of an afternoon that there really *is* a God, and that God can come to us through a vividly living Christ. I saw in an almost mystical flash of insight that God's life and power dissolve death. I sensed that I could live the rest of my life "within" God. The recognition that Christianity was *true* floored me. I took a step toward God that day. That step, and miles of walking since that day, have set the trajectory of my life on a profoundly different course than I might have taken otherwise.

I move more consciously with God. Prayer plays a significant part in my life. It feels like a lifeline to God. Talking with other people about faith is a gift and a joy. Churches amaze me. They can be communities of learning, of spirituality—stunning focal points of serving others. Sometimes churches drive me a little nuts, because it's so easy for them to drift like rowboats on a pond, bobbing in eddies of muted niceness and respectability, rather than heeling in the wind like clipper ships cutting through waves, sailing into mysteries of ever-deepening layers of reality.

But I get over it. I love the potential churches embody. And oh, I have *so* much respect for what God can do with groups of people who are willing to take some steps toward letting God use them. That's when people and churches are at our best!

I know one thing: God exists. Walking through my life with God and with other Christians has been an adventure for 30 years. It's available to everyone if we'll do a couple of simple things: talk with some other people about what really matters in our lives; pray; explore faith traditions, writings and ideas; and be willing to see new things.

Who knows what can happen next if we'll do three simple things:

- talk for real
- pray
- explore new ideas

If you choose, you can make the next four weeks your experiment in Christian prayer and community. Here's the choice: Are you willing to talk about the things that matter in your life? Will you try some different ways of praying? Will you work with a few readings from the Bible? Will you talk with a small group of other people about what you think and are learning about your life? ...God? ...your

"Yes, I remember that conversation with you. It was fun and interesting and challenging. I was surprised when you told me later of your personal encounter with God. Whenever I read that passage in 1st Corinthians about Paul planting, Apollos watering but God giving the growth, I always think of you. I may have planted, but God definitely gave the growth, since I was totally surprised to see it. I remember thinking it was a conversion from intellectual curiosity to personal understanding."

—Hilary's 2009 recollection of talking with Martha Grace about faith in Spain

hopes? ...faith? (Whatever these things are to you?) This process works best when the participants have very different backgrounds and spiritual experiences.

Telling the truth and talking for real can be scary. Sometimes you wonder if it isn't better **not** to talk about the things that bother you, or that you wonder about. A lot of us assume it's better to "let sleeping dogs lie." It's a little risky to let people get to know you. And yet, sometimes it's better to talk honestly if the setting is safe and people all agree to hold the conversations in confidence.

We Live in Invisible Currents:

A woman packages the tools and equipment needed for surgeries at Emory University Hospital. She looks at the patients' names, packs the instruments the surgical teams may need, and prays for them and their surgeries. She told a chaplain that she had established this routine 40 years ago. The chaplain interviewed hospital employees and discovered that most of them did the same thing. No one knew.[3]

Many parts of the Bible resonate with depth and truth. If I had to pick one of the most important spots in the Bible, it might be the time when Jesus told his followers, "If you continue in my word, you are truly my disciples; and you will know the truth, and the truth will make you free." (John 8:31–32) There's another spot where one of the greatest writers of the New Testament, Paul of Tarsus, talks about "speaking the truth in love." (Ephesians 4:15)

Those are my assumptions about this group. We need to speak the truth, in love—gently, clearly, knowing that none of us ever has the whole picture about anything. We understand so little about even our **own** lives. The **unconscious** parts must be like the **big, hidden** part of the iceberg! Even our "truest," most deeply held beliefs, ideas, and feelings don't encompass the whole truth. So we need to speak with each other "in love," as Paul says. We must listen to each other, knowing that no matter how right we are, we each only understand a small part of what's real and true. This isn't relativism; it's the reality of the human situation. When we recognize how limited we all are, it's easier to speak humbly and kindly with each other.

People who have studied **Unbinding the Gospel** together have discovered that God will move them into deeper layers of understanding and truth if they speak honestly and kindly, pray, and try to take just one or two "next steps" in spiritual growth. In Jesus' words, the "truth will set you free."

If **your** group chooses, these presuppositions can become the foundation upon which your group is based. Speak honestly. Speak and listen in love. Be open when the Spirit prompts you to be. God will bring about the right results.

If you don't usually connect with a church, THANK you for your courage and willingness to explore something new. Each chapter gives you a short bit to read and think about before you meet with your group. **Unbinding Your Soul** also includes a personal prayer journal, with daily prayer exercises for three weeks. You and the person who invited you to be part of the group might choose to be prayer partners during these next weeks.

Those of you who <u>are</u> connected with a church–THANK <u>*You*</u> for your courage and willingness to be open to something new *and to talk about it!* You're willing to talk out loud about something that you've probably been warned to keep private. Grandad *lived* his faith beautifully, but when I was a girl, I didn't know what motivated him. Had Hilary not arrived on the scene and actually spoken out loud about Christianity, I might have missed it. I wish Grandad had told me what he thought about this one area where he was silent.

The thing is, I didn't ask Grandad, either! I would give anything to be able to talk with him about his faith now. I missed it. It's so odd, because I've spoken one-on-one with probably 2,000 people about their faith–people with all *types* of faith experiences. I've learned so much from each one. Millions of people believe what Grandmother Reese thought. Millions more are like Grandad. Lots are somewhere in the middle. It's wonderful when people can get past the "don't talk about sex, money, politics or religion" taboo. We all live in deep places in our souls. It *matters* that we share the quiet, hidden, motivating forces and wonderings with other people. Whatever we believe, it matters that we talk! Why wait for someone fascinating to bring it up? We could ask.

> "A friend at church once commented, 'What I want the most is to be truly known, but that's what I fear the most too.' She and another woman are probably the only people at church I would tell about what is really going on in my life, which probably says more about me than my church. But, still, what good is this faith community stuff otherwise?"

My husband's father was a quiet man, a Marine captain, a Pilgrim descendant, raised in flinty New England. He used to quote, "Better to remain silent and be thought a fool than to speak out and remove all doubt."[4] Most Christians ignore this advice in every area of their lives *except* the religious sphere. I *urge* you to disregard it during your group's meetings. (Younger readers: scratch out ~~disregard it,~~ insert "blow it off.") Give yourself a pass! Just blurt stuff right out there. Everybody'll be doing it.

---

[1]Stephen G. Bloom and Peter Feldstein, *The Oxford Project* (New York: Welcome Books, 2008). Quotes from Oxford Project story, CNN.com, October 28, 2008.

[2]Frances Hodgson Burnett, *Little Lord Fauntleroy* (New York: Scribners, 1886).

[3]Janet Lutz, Story Corps account of hospital-wide interviews conducted while she was chaplain at Emory University Hospital, reported on CNN.com, December 18, 2008.

[4]Russ' dad used to attribute the quote to Abraham Lincoln, but Benjamin Franklin, Mark Twain, George Eliot and the Bible (Proverbs 17) are also suspects. Whoever said it first, it has stuck in the culture of our churches!

GROUP DISCUSSION_____

1. Introduce yourselves. Talk a bit. Why are you here? What do you hope to get out of this time?

2. Talk about the group and what you want this process to be. Review the covenant, page 10, stressing the importance of confidentiality.

3. What did you think about chapter 1, *Get Started?*

4. What's your reaction to the thought of talking about faith issues? Check all the statements that you are saying inside your head:

Your Group's Foundations:

- Speak honestly.
- Speak and listen in love.
- Explore new ideas.
- Maintain confidentiality.

❏ I'm feeling a little queasy. I'm considering bolting for that side door right about now.

❏ My beloved spouse makes me talk and pray every once in awhile. It's part of marriage, like apologizing.

❏ I'm with Grandmother Reese. I don't buy this Christianity thing.

❏ I've been in church all my life. I love God, but I don't want to look pushy or offend anyone.

❏ I'm not sure there *is* a God.

❏ I've always wondered about spiritual things.

❏ Wow, did I get burned by a church. It's a horrible story!

❏ I'm cautiously optimistic.

❏ I'm so excited. I have been looking for a place to be able to talk absolutely bluntly about the things that really matter in my life. I'm in!

So, talk a little! Talk a lot. What do you think?

TRY SOME PRAYER_____

Pass out prayer candles

Give each person a prayer candle. (See description at the end of chapter 5, page 66.)

Test out a prayer exercise

Take a look at the prayer journals. Go over the key points of *Using Your Prayer Journal* (pages 123–131). Decide who will work together as prayer partners. I suggest being a prayer partner with the person who invited you into the group, but adjust as needed for your group. Arrange your chairs so that you and your prayer partner are sitting close to another couple of prayer partners.

Do the first prayer day (Week A, Day 1, [page 12]) together as a group. Help each other find the places in your Bibles. Tomorrow when you do this same exercise, you'll read it by yourself and do it in your own house. Today, read the scripture by yourselves, silently. Then let your facilitator guide your whole group through the exercise. Follow along with the Bible passage by reading it as the facilitator reads it or just listen. Do whatever helps you absorb it most clearly.

DISCUSSION

In groups of four *(two pairs of prayer partners)*:

Say something about what the prayer was like. Did any light bulbs go on? Which parts inspired you? …frustrated you? Did any surprises or realizations emerge during the readings? …during the silence? What are you going to think about now?

Re-gather in the full group

Discuss how the prayer went, what you learned. What do you wonder about? Did anyone's comments surprise you?

Questions? Everyone ready to start on Week A, Day 1 of the prayers tomorrow? Exchange phone numbers so you can call someone if you get a great idea and want to talk.

Close in prayer

Ask God to bless each of you, your families, this time together and your times of prayer this week.

> This is a pretty humble process. It isn't rocket science. It's spiritual growth. We trust that God will bless our lives and take us to the next deeper level if we'll talk honestly with each other, listen carefully and respectfully to each other, study bits of the Bible and pray.

A CHALLENGE

I'd like to throw out a little challenge to you. How would you like to interview someone fascinating within the next two weeks? I'd love to be able to ask Grandmother **and** Grandad about their ideas and perceptions of God, now that I'm an adult. What if you were to talk with someone you love, or someone you admire, and asked them what they thought about faith issues? My experience with thousands of people is that we all love to be asked to talk about our lives, what we think, what we've experienced. People are honored to be asked. Wouldn't you be? You'll find a suggested form for these interviews (different forms for people who normally don't go to church and those who do) at www.GraceNet.info / Download Resources / Public Downloads / Interviews. (Facilitators, download it for everyone, will you?)

Okay! Good job, everybody! Now go get ice cream or something. Have a great week. Enjoy the prayer exercises. If something isn't clear, or if you just want to talk about something, call your prayer partner or someone else in the group who looked nice. See you back soon!

"I haven't talked with anyone about what I really believe. I've gone to church sometimes but I've never talked about what I think is bogus, or what I really wonder about. What have I been waiting for?"

—man invited to join an *Unbinding Your Heart* group

GROUP COVENANT

1. ***Confidentiality.*** I agree to hold everything said in this group in confidence. I will not repeat anything personal another group member says in the group, or during a private conversation outside the group. I can, of course, talk with people outside the group about how my experience of the group is affecting me, but will talk about it in ways that won't reveal another group member's confidence.

2. ***Participation.*** I'll participate in the four group meetings and arrive on time.

3. ***Preparation.*** I'll read the chapter before we meet and do the prayer exercises each day. If a prayer exercise seems annoying or stupid one day, I'll think about why it bothers me, write down why, and pray some other way. (Or just try it!)

Notes

The Main Point

Scripture: Isaiah 40:28–31

Are you sitting in your chair, with Bible, pen, candle and matches at hand? All right! Light your candle if you want to. Sit quietly and calm down a little. Take a few deep breaths and relax. When you exhale, imagine that you're letting go of all the things you're thinking about. Now read the Scripture passage. What phrases or words strike you as important? Which ones do you like? Write them down here or underline them in your Bible.

Isaiah was a prophet who lived more than 700 years before Jesus' birth (about 740 to 700 B.C.) Prophets tell people what's true about the world. They make the spiritual equivalent of that "ah..eh..eh..eh..eeeehhhhhhhh" noise when someone gets out of line. Isaiah lived with a vivid sense of God's power, love and mercy. He stressed how safe we are when we trust God. Think about what Isaiah says here about two things:

(1) What's God like?
(2) What are people like when we rely on God?

Read the passage again. Do you see answers to these two questions?

Read Isaiah's words one more time. If you're alone, read them out loud. What phrases seem most important this time as you hear them? Write down the words that "grab" you. What trains of thought are you starting on as you think about these important words or images? Do you believe that God exists? How does Isaiah's picture of God seem? Has God ever given you power when you felt weak? Can you imagine God renewing your strength so that you can mount up with wings, like eagles? Write your reactions to the passage here. What do you wonder about? Is there anything in yourself or your life that you'd like to change?

Notes, drawings, thoughts:

If you'd like to say a prayer, try this *(say it out loud, whisper it, or "think" it in your head):*
God, I can't imagine what you are like, but please help me get a better sense of you during these next four weeks. Thank you for the other people in this group. Will you please give each of us what we need during these four weeks together? Thank you. Amen.

Everybody Has a Story

Scripture: John 8:1–11

Light your candle. Get calm. Take a few deep breaths. When you exhale, imagine that you're letting go of all the normal things you think about. Now read the scripture passage for today, slowly. Do you get the picture? A woman had an affair. The Jewish law (the "law of Moses") dictated a mandatory minimum sentence: death by stoning. A group of by-the-book literalists ("scribes and Pharisees") tried to trick Jesus by saying, "Jesus, the Bible says she should be stoned, but what do *you* think?" Perhaps they thought he'd say not to punish her. Then they could hold press conferences accusing him of being soft on crime. Jesus didn't answer directly. He acknowledged the punishment. In essence, he said "Go ahead, stone her. She earned it. Anyone who hasn't sinned can throw the first stone."

Look what happened. *They* all had a story, too—hidden or forgotten for a moment, but right there, on their consciences, in their pasts. They left. Jesus looked directly at the woman and told her he didn't condemn her. Now—don't do it again.

I heard a man say, "We need to be gentle with each other. Everybody's got a story." What's yours? What is the one thing in your life you'd love to take back, to undo? …the thing that might get people palming rocks to throw at you? Which memory makes you flinch? We all have one.

Would you be willing to whisper it now to Jesus? Tell him about the memory in your mind, even if you don't really believe he's there. He sees your sin for exactly what it is, unvarnished. He sees it even more clearly than you do. He won't condemn you. Tell him how sorry you are. See if you can feel his hand on your head, blessing you, taking the pain and the guilt away. Now go into your day. Start fresh.

Notes, drawings, thoughts:

Quote: Be kind, because everyone you meet is fighting a mighty battle.

Philo of Alexandria, Egypt, 1st century

Prayer: Jesus, I hardly dare look in your face and tell you this: _____
_____. Please forgive me and help me begin again. Amen.

Count Your Blessings

Scripture: Genesis 18:1–8

Sit comfortably for a minute. Read the scripture carefully, a couple of times. Sarah and Abraham are the original "parents" of the Jewish people. Three men visit them as they are camped near an oasis. Sarah and Abraham are herders. It later turns out that the men are really angels, messengers from God. But Abraham and Sarah don't know that. Do you see the extravagant hospitality Sarah and Abraham offer—water to wash, rest, a banquet? Think about the gift this couple gave the men.

We don't think about it, or see it, very often, but people (and God) give us gifts every day. Our very lives are gifts. People bless us, and we're so busy, we just blow by it and don't even recognize a blessing when someone hands it to us! People let us cut into a line of traffic. A greeter at Wal-Mart holds a door or gives you a cart. Maybe you don't get the speeding ticket you earned! Someone catches your child swiping M & Ms™ and talks with her! You have a job. You are *out* of work, but can volunteer at the animal shelter. Someone talks to you at the gym. Lunch with your friends at school is fun. Someone sends you a thank-you note. You get to spend an hour reading.

Here's the field trip challenge: Carry a 3 x 5 card in your pocket today. Every time a person, or circumstances, or God gives you a "gift" (blesses you somehow), write a short note about it. Then whisper "thank you" to God. Say "thank you" directly if there's another person involved. Then ask God to bless that person too! Look at your card at the end of the day. Paper clip it right here. What do you think? Are you blessed?

Notes, drawings, thoughts:

Prayer: Oh, holy God—help me to be sensitive to all the blessings in my life. I pray now for each of the people who gave me some gift today. [Think about each person, picture them in your head, then whisper their name aloud to God. Ask God to bless them.] Thank you, God, for being the instigator of all these blessings! Amen.

Now *You* Can Give

Scripture: Luke 20:45–21:4

Light your candle. You know the drill. Calm down. Concentrate and slowly read the scripture. Do you see what's going on? Jesus ("he") was teaching by the Temple in Jerusalem. (Only one wall of the Temple remains today. The "Wailing Wall," the "Western Wall," is holy ground for all Jews.) Jesus told his disciples, his primary followers, to be careful of the scribes, many of whom were wealthy, hypocritical leaders who loved everyone's admiration and respect, but didn't have much real holiness. Along came a poor widow. She put two tiny copper coins into the collection boxes (the "treasury") in the Temple. She gave her food money to God. If you look at it as a percentage of what she had, it was an enormous gift.

Review your 3 x 5 card from yesterday. Think or say "thank you" to God for all of the blessings. Now ask God if God will show you something *you* could give today. Don't decide yourself. Ask. Sit quietly in the silence now and ask God (or Jesus, or the Spirit, whichever feels most comfortable) to give you an idea of something you could do for someone else. Sit for a while. Write down any ideas that come into your mind.

Buy an extra sandwich to give to a homeless person? Donate money to a shelter? Secretly help someone who lost their job? Is someone at school being bullied? Could you help stop it? God might love it if you visited your lonely neighbor, or called someone on the phone. Take treats to your kid's class, or to the nursing home. Here's a thought: If you give something to anyone, hold it in your hands for a moment—the sandwich, tray of cupcakes, envelope with a check, the phone before you dial. Ask (think in your mind) God to bless the gift and bless the person who receives it. Have fun!

Notes, drawings, thoughts:

Prayer:

May the road rise to meet you.
May the wind be always at your back.
May the sun shine warm upon your face.
And rains fall soft upon your fields.
And until we meet again,
May God hold you in the hollow of His hand.

Ancient Irish Blessing

Prayer Partners

Scripture: Romans 16

(Select your meeting day to fit your schedules. If you meet on Day 4, do Day 4's prayer exercise on Day 5. You'll figure it out! Just aim for a time about halfway between group meetings.)

Paul of Tarsus, sometimes called "Saint" Paul, wrote these words. He was a scholarly Jew. He didn't know Jesus during Jesus' lifetime, but Paul became one of the main leaders of the new movement of Jesus' followers that turned into Christianity. He crisscrossed the Mediterranean basin from Jerusalem, through modern Turkey, Greece and Macedonia, to Rome, teaching and founding communities. His letters to these little churches make up a huge part of the New Testament.

I love Romans 16. First, it looks like just a list of people that I'd tend to skim over lightly. But I like that 2000 years later, you can still tell how much Paul respected and loved these people. Prisca and Aquila "risked their necks" for Paul (see verse 3). Look at verse 13. Rufus was Paul's friend, but it looks as if Rufus' mom loved Paul too. She probably made the boys' dinner, listened while they talked, and gave them sage advice while they ate. Maybe she rolled her eyes when Paul wedged his muddy sandals against the rungs of the clean kitchen chairs. All I'm saying is, Paul wasn't a Christian on his own—these people were close friends in one of the very first churches, about 15 years after Jesus was crucified.*

Churches are still filled with heroic, loving people who have fun together. *We* can start with prayer partners. Meet today with *your* prayer partner. Talk about what has happened as you've done these prayers this week. How did your group meeting affect you? Did any of the prayer exercises make you crazy? Did you learn anything? What do you wonder about? What have you really liked? Help each other any way you can. Just talk about what's going on.

Notes, lists, drawings, ideas:

Prayer: God, please bless my prayer partner. Bless the people in my group and all of their families. Thank you for this time with these people. Let me see and learn whatever is best for me to learn next. Amen.

---

*Fred Craddock, beloved Disciples preacher, biblical scholar, professor and pastor preached a series of 12 sermons on Romans in Canada, probably in the 1970s. They're the most powerful sermons I've ever heard. He spoke of Paul and Rufus' mother in a way I'll never forget. I can't find these sermons, which were on tape. If anyone knows where I could find a set, let me know!

Review & Think

Read. Have you read chapter 2 so you're ready for tomorrow's group meeting?

Review. Think back over your week of prayer. Reread your favorite scripture from the week. Review your notes, lists, insights. How is your prayer life going? Review *Using Your Prayer Journal* on page 123. Which ideas do you need to pay particular attention to this week? Take some notes.

Then, answer two questions:

Question 1. What are the most important things you've learned/discovered/remembered this week?

Question 2. What do you wonder about?

Prayer: Talk to God. Sit in silence for a bit. Listen. Amen.

From a Midwest, university church. The building is stone, elegant and neo-gothic:

"Most of our members are highly educated and highly rational. Prayer hasn't been a strong suit for either the congregation or for me (the pastor). We've started praying seriously since our all-church study of **Unbinding Your Heart,** *and the light went on for me.*

Several Jews and Muslims have started worshipping with us. We are overwhelmed that they feel free to worship God with us and with each other. Last Sunday, a bedraggled, drunk, homeless man (another first for us!) walked in at the beginning of the worship service. He sat in the pew, weaving back and forth. I was already in the pulpit. I saw two leaders in the congregation in back, huddling over whether they were going to have to remove the man, and ask him to come with them into another room.

Ahmet walked over, in his turban, with his long robe sweeping about his legs. He sat down next to the homeless man. He put his arm around the man and helped him sit upright during the whole service. God's at work."

CHAPTER 2

Surround Sounds & God Sightings

My family goes to a cabin in the Chippewa National Forest in far northern Minnesota. It's 50 miles south of Canada. The post office is ten miles to the west, the grocery 10 miles north. Our daughters love the woods, but they have a tough time adjusting to all the noises of the great, "silent" forest when they come north. We hear this kind of report as they straggle down from upstairs near noon, in sweat suits, flip-flops and tangly hair:

Daughter #1: "Okay, so I was going to sleep, then this **wind** came through the window. I mean, it's like **June** and it's freezing and I'm in my sweats and **socks**. But I put on another quilt and the comforter, so it got all cuddly, and I started falling asleep. **Then** I heard this horrible whoooooooooooooooo sound, and I woke up and thought, '**Whoa**, that scared me to death!' But I realized it was an owl, which was actually pretty cool. It was just **really** loud. So I started drifting back to sleep and then I heard like bulls making this really big sound at the lake [frogs]."

Daughter #2: "Well, **I** woke up when I heard this goofy hahahahahaha sound that was like somebody demented **laughing** in this totally creepy way [deer]. Then I couldn't sleep for like a **really** long time. I just kept **hearing** things making spooky **creaking** noises, really loudly [trees]. **Then** I heard this **WOLF**–actually, it was a **lot** of wolves. So I jumped up and slammed the window shut and pulled down the shades because I knew if I didn't, some **Mad Lumberjack** would come through the window and **get** me."

We're all wired a little differently. We have different backgrounds. We live in different situations. We change through the course of our lives. So we will see God from where we are and who we are. We'll perceive God with the intellectual, emotional and neurological equipment we each have!

Daughter #1: "Okay. Like, we'd better settle down." So they popped Skittles,™ drank cocoa, made chocolate chip pancakes with syrup, and lemonade and watched chainsaw movies to relax.

But the *moral* of the story is that three nights later, nobody hears a thing. They just sleep. We've adapted. Frogs, deer, owls, wolves and any Mad Lumberjacks (we've yet to have a confirmed sighting) are *still* out there. We just don't hear them anymore.

God's "Out There" and "In Here"

Okay—that's how I think it is with God. God's all around us. We are so used to the sounds around us that we don't hear a thing. (Let's get clear here. I'm *not* calling God a Mad Lumberjack—that was just part of the Girls in the Woods story. We'd better not stretch this analogy too far.) God is huge, infinite, through time, across the ages, and God cares for each of us in the tiniest details of our lives. That's true, and we're swimming in it! We live in the very midst of an awe-filled, overwhelmingly glorious, creative world, and the presence of God is all around us, knocking on the doors of our hearts.

The core of what Christians believe is that God is "out there" *and* that God is "in here." God offers to live inside us and in the midst of groups of people who want to be awake to divine presence. The whole church is based on a deep belief that Jesus, who lived 2000 years ago, *is* God. We believe that Jesus is alive right now and active in the world. Different parts of the church would describe that basic belief a little bit differently. Here's the key point: Jesus and his Spirit will show us God, will help us grow closer to God, more united in God, and into infinite and eternal life with God.

This reality lies at the core of the faith: God loves us more than we can ever understand. Christians live their whole lives trying to know a little more of this love that can change, heal, forgive, and fix us individually. Christians live their whole lives trying to be part of this power that can reshape history, heal neighborhoods, change nations.

How Do You *Know*?

How in the world can we, as goofy, messed up people even *begin* to get a glimpse of the huge, infinite glory God keeps trying to show us? We can say that Jesus is alive and right here, that God created the world and is breathing life into it, and that God's Spirit can guide, comfort and empower us daily. You can *say* that, but we can't *see* them. How do you *know*???

God loves us more than we can ever understand. Christians live their whole lives trying to know a little more of this love that can change, and heal, and forgive, and fix us individually. Christians live their whole lives trying to be part of this power that can reshape history, heal neighborhoods, change nations.

No simple answer satisfies that big a question. We're all wired a little differently. We have different backgrounds, different situations, and we change through the course of our lives. So we will see God from **where** we are and **who** we are. We'll perceive God with our own intellectual, emotional and neurological equipment. New medical research shows that prayer "sculpts" your brain the way weight-lifting sculpts your muscles. Your brain will change if you pray, even for short periods of time, for a couple of months.[1]

The bottom line is, we'll all see God, and God's activity, a little differently. We can become neurologically more like great prayer masters if we pray. Who knew? Probably most of the spiritual teachers for thousands of years!

How do we know we're seeing God and not making up religious experience out of our own fevered imaginations? Different people perceive God differently. Some people have very visceral senses of God through prayer, as they go through their day. It changes during their lives, sometimes more intense, sometimes gone for a while. Others don't believe there **is** a God, but have occasional, numinous moments sitting on the bank of a stream, or singing Mozart, or hunting in the woods in October, as sunlight filters through orange, yellow and red leaves.

Have you ever walked into a cathedral, sat quietly and experienced a sense of awe? …of how small you are, how short your life is? Have you ever sensed something bigger, resonant, "behind" that awe?

Some people see God in what could look like coincidences. You'll need something specific—a sense of direction in your life, $500 for rent, the right music teacher for your daughter. At exactly the time, sometimes with the oddest and most elaborate coincidences, what you really need (possibly not what you **thought** you needed) appears.

Some people—artists, cooks, software designers, engineers, athletes, scholars, doctors, mechanics, dog trainers, scientists, writers, musicians—can feel the movement of God's Spirit in a creative process. You think and wonder and plan and work, then you get stuck. Suddenly something breaks free and you're cookin'! You can feel as if you're rafting through rapids, swirling around rocks through a current, in a flow you didn't even know was there.

Many people read something in the Bible, sometimes a paragraph they've read 100 times before, and suddenly the words gleam off the page—filled with a meaning and importance the reader never

"The circumstances for my God-sighting happened long ago, but I only recently recognized it as the power of God at work at the time. My father died in 1981…six times. He was resuscitated, made it through surgery and lived a healthy life for an additional fifteen years. While I sat in the ICU waiting room that night, a virtual stranger came up to me and said, "Our church is filled with people tonight who are praying for your father." It isn't until now that I'm praying earnestly for others that I begin to appreciate the power that Christian love and faith sharing can bring to a person, a need, a situation. I was **in** the God-moment then, but I had the God-sighting **now** as a result of knowing Him better through our study."

—*Methodist in Virginia*

understood before. The words "carry" God's meaning, or God's truth on their backs. That's part of what people are talking about when they describe the Bible as "inspired." (The word "inspired" comes from a Greek word that infers that the Spirit "breathes" God's very life into the book's words.)

Some people pray or talk with a friend and an idea falls into place—everything you thought you knew about the world reshuffles into a new framework.

Many charismatic and Pentecostal Christians feel the Holy Spirit inside them, guiding them step-by-step through the day. They feel it physically, often as words of prayer and praise of God, bubbling up inside them.

Many of us have felt a touch of awe and amazement during a candlelight Christmas Eve service. The dark enfolds us with our families—children and parents and dear Christian brothers and sisters. As the candlelight flickers on faces, the dark ceiling of the sanctuary stretches upward, the cross beckons, the Holy Family radiates love, we feel something deep that connects us with it all.

Others sit in a hospital room, waiting with a dear one, and feel a whisper of comfort, an almost physical sense of love and hope and certainty.

Occasionally a person will appear in your life at *just* the right time, bearing *exactly* the right message.

People perceive God's presence or activity in these and many other ways. The curious fact is that God is working whether we have a feeling or sense of presence, or not. A visceral experience of God's presence is wonderful, but certainly isn't necessary. God is present and active whether we feel it or not.

Mother Teresa of Calcutta, one of the great saints of our times, served the dying and the poor in India for almost 50 years. She braved the streets during a riot as a young woman to get food for the students in her school. She showed amazing dedication to God from her youth. She radiated joy. She experienced a vivid, mysterious, mystical sense of Jesus' presence as a young woman. Then a spiritual "dryness" set in. Mother Teresa could no longer "feel" Christ's presence.[2] She kept going, reading scripture, serving the poor, praying for hours, feeling nothing, rarely sensing God's presence, yet always smiling and loving people out of her love for Jesus.

She experienced almost 50 years of spiritual dryness. Yet tens of thousands of people caught glimpses of Jesus' face in her wrinkled face, felt Christ's presence as they saw her serve the dying in India.

"The golf buddies can't believe I'm praying 30 minutes a day. Me either, but I'm way calmer at work and with my family. That's saying a lot. I lost 70% of my personal retirement this quarter because of the bank failures and stock market nosedive. I'm getting a sense of the Holy Spirit in my life I never had before. This prayer is crucial."

She felt nothing but a call to serve and a love for Jesus and the poor. She inspired millions. ***They saw Christ's love*** radiating out to the world through her tiny, sari-clad figure.

"Thin Places"

It's always different. Different people perceive God in different ways. No matter how powerfully God overwhelms us with perceptions of God's presence, we still only understand miniscule bits of the majesty, power and love of the infinite God. We live in a world that God is saturating with holy presence. We just haven't learned to see it, or we're too used to it, or we skim by it as we race on to the next thing in our lives.

People in a Methodist church in Virginia are trying to get more conscious of "God Sightings." The sidebar quote on page 21 comes from one of their members. Another member, a retired Army officer in the congregation, told me about a 12-year-old boy who "described about how he felt when he saw a litter of kittens being born. This boy was so brave to get up in front of 200 people and talk like that. We were all really touched. He was so cute."

At the end of his talk to the church, the boy concluded, "Just look around. God sightings are all ***over*** the place! God's doing things everywhere! ...all the time!" The boy saw God as he watched the kittens being born. The people in the congregation caught a glimpse of God at work in the boy.

Seeing God is up to God. Yet we can ask to be ready, and to be awake when it happens. Have you read or seen *The Lion, the Witch and the Wardrobe* by C.S. Lewis?[3] A child walks through the back of a "wardrobe," a freestanding closet, and finds Narnia, another world, filled with mystery and with God. Harry Potter, Hermione and Ron board the train to their school, Hogwarts, on Platform 9 3/4 in King's Cross Station in London.[4] Hogwarts students and their families pass through a brick wall to the platform. Normal Londoners don't even know the platform's ***there***.

Seeing God is like that—a whole world of truth, power, love and glory is right there, but as St. Paul says, we see it "in a mirror dimly," or "through a [looking] glass darkly" (1 Corinthians 13:12). We can't see God clearly. We can't make anything happen. And yet a whole world of God's truth, and action and understanding exists just on the other side of that mirror. Sometimes, if we ask, if we prepare ourselves by talking with each other, by reading scripture, by praying and waiting, God shows us a glimpse.

Seeing God is up to God. Yet we can ask to be ready, and to be awake when it happens. A whole world of truth, power, love and glory is right there, on the other side of the mirror. Sometimes, if we ask, if we prepare ourselves by talking with each other, by reading scripture, by praying and waiting, God shows us a glimpse.

A friend of mine from Indianapolis sent me an e-mail this week from New York. He'd gone there for a couple of days of meetings. He tried to get in touch with a young woman whose advice he wanted on a crucial decision, but hadn't been able to reach her. He slipped into a Starbucks to grab some coffee between meetings, still stewing over the decision. The woman he had tried to call walked into the Starbucks in Manhattan. They had a wonderful conversation. The woman's advice clarified my friend's take on the situation. He e-mailed, "It is moments like these when I realize how 'hooked up' everything really is! It is already my theology, but every so often we find ourselves in one of these 'thin places.' It is just amazing, and wonderful, and such a confirmation of faith."

The details of the "thin places" rarely impress. The "stuff" that happens almost doesn't matter, but these moments when we slip through the back of the wardrobe into Narnia impress us with a sense of overwhelming importance, and of confirmation. We sense that these inconsequential coincidences reveal a truth larger than the world.

We live in a world that God permeates with meaning, and with Godself.

We can't **make** God appear. We **can** ask to see, to hear, to begin to become aware of whatever God would like to show us.

> We live in a world that God permeates with meaning, and with Godself.
> We can't **make** God appear. We **can** ask to see, to hear, to begin to become aware of whatever God would like to show us.

---

[1]Barbara Bradley Hagerty, *Prayer May Reshape Your Brain…And Your Reality*, www.NPR.org, May 20, 2009.

[2]See *Come Be My Light: The Private Writings of the Saint of Calcutta*, ed. Brian Kolodiejchuk (New York: Doubleday, 2007).

[3]C. S. Lewis, *The Lion, the Witch and the Wardrobe* (Bel Air, Calif.: HarperFesitval, 2005).

[4]J. K. Rowling, *Harry Potter and the Sorcerer's Stone*, 10th Anniversary ed. (New York: Scholastic Publishing, 2008).

GROUP DISCUSSION _____

1. Open with prayer.

2. How did the prayer exercises go this week? Let each person describe the most important thing they want to tell the group. (See page 17 of your journal to remind yourself of your prayer review yesterday.) What did you learn this week? What amazed you? Confused you?

3. Discussion: Any thoughts about the chapter you just read? Reactions? Questions? What did you love? What made you crazy? Talk a little!

GROUP EXERCISE _____

Divide into groups of three. Sit quietly for a couple of minutes to get a bit more centered. In the silence, ask God to show you some story of a "God sighting," a "thin place," a moment of transparency when you recognized the presence or activity of God. You may not have recognized it as a God sighting at the time, but ask God to show you something now.

Take four minutes each to tell your stories. As the other people in your group tell their stories, listen quietly—don't ask questions or say anything. Pray for them as they talk—that they'll have exactly the right words to express something important. Pray that God will bless them in precisely the way they need to be blessed.

(Facilitator—let everyone know when the person speaking only has a minute left of their four minutes. Then tell the group when the four minutes is up and it's time to move to the next person's story.)

Your Group's Foundations:

- Speak honestly.
- Speak and listen in love.
- Explore new ideas.
- Maintain confidentiality.

Group Interaction

What happened as you talked? …as you listened? What did you learn?

How do your stories and the ideas in chapter 2 connect?

Prayer

Close in prayer, using the Prayer Triads on page 41. Skip the prayer triads until next week if you're completely out of time. End with a brief blessing by one of the facilitators. Pray that you will each be open to God and that each person will be able to see what God would like to show you during the next week.

The Lord's Prayer

Scripture: Matthew 6:5–15

Light your candle, relax, and read what Jesus taught us about praying. Read it a second time. This prayer unites the church across the world and across two thousand years. It's called the Lord's Prayer (Christians call Jesus "Lord.")

An estimated two billion people prayed this prayer on Easter Day 2009, in hundreds of languages. Imagine what Matthew, Luke, Paul, and Rufus' mother would have thought if they had known how many people would pray together the prayer Jesus taught us, 2000 years after they all lived.)

Look what Jesus says about prayer. Read it carefully. Underline the specific things Jesus tells us about the way to pray (look at verses 5-8). Now look at the prayer he gave us. He wanted us to pray for the largest things, and for the smallest. We praise God in the highest heaven. We ask that God's kingdom come on earth, that God's will be done. Those are all huge things. *And* we're to pray for the most specific details in our lives–that we have enough to eat, for forgiveness, and that we forgive others and that we be safe from evil. The biggest things, the tiniest things–Jesus tells us God exists and rules on the most enormous, unfathomable layers of reality *and* that God cares intimately about the tiniest details of our lives. God meets us everywhere.

Think about the prayer. What thoughts occur to you? Pray it slowly, thinking about each phrase. (You could pray the version in Matthew, or use the one listed below, which is traditional in many churches.) Pray it again. You're moving in sync with billions of people who have lived through 20 centuries.

Notes, drawings, lists, thoughts:

Prayer:

Our Father, who art in heaven

Hallowed be thy name

Thy kingdom come, thy will be done

On earth, as it is in heaven.

Give us this day our daily bread

And forgive us our sins, as we forgive those who sin against us *[or forgive us our debts, as we forgive our debtors; **or** forgive us our trespasses as we forgive those who trespass against us].*

And lead us not into temptation, but deliver us from evil

For thine is the Kingdom, and the power and the glory forever. Amen.

A God Sighting (The Burning Bush)

Scripture: Exodus 3:1–12

Sit calmly. Breathe. Read this passage from Exodus, the second book in the Old Testament. Some of Sarah and Abraham's descendants went to Egypt to find food. Generations later, they were slaves. Exodus is the story of God bringing the Jews out of Egypt and back to their Holy Land, modern Israel. (The word "exodus" means "going out" or "departure"). Moses led the people through 40 years in the wilderness and to the very edge of the Promised Land, territory God promised Abraham for his descendants. Chapter 3 tells the story of God communicating with Moses when Moses was about 40 years old.

What do you see about God in this passage? Go through it carefully. Read aloud the words that God says. What is God like? Can you write down words to describe God? Imagine describing God as if God were a person. Try it.

Then think about the relationship God has with the Jews. God sees their sufferings (verse 7) and has a loving plan for their future (verse 8). Look at Moses' reaction to God: "Who am I to go to Pharaoh, and lead the people out of Egypt?" (It's the old "I couldn't do that! I'm just a kid" response!) God answers Moses' "Who am I" question with, "I will be with you." *Moses can be who God is calling him to be because God will be there.*

Reread the passage. Close your eyes. Imagine you're out on a hillside and see a burning bush. What does it feel like to see a bush burst into flames and to hear a voice out of it? Does God say anything to you? What do you feel like? What do you say? Hear God saying, "I will be with you" directly to you. How do you feel? Write a bit about it here.

Notes, drawings, thoughts, insights:

Prayer: Oh Creator of the Universe—I can't even imagine you. Your majesty overwhelms me. Please let me see the tiny portion of your glory that I can understand. Please use me to do whatever you would like me to do for people you love. I can't do anything truly important on my own. Help me to trust I can do anything I need to because you promise to be with me. Amen.

Rocks in Your Backpack

Scripture: Matthew 11:25–30

Supplies: A backpack, shopping bag with straps, or big purse; rocks, or bricks, or books or weights—heavy things that will fit in the bag

Light your candle. Get centered. Read the scripture. Jesus is talking. Do you know what a yoke is? It's the wooden beam that goes between a pair of oxen—it's what the plow is attached to.

What is Jesus saying here? To go to him with our burdens and he'll give us rest? Could Jesus be saying that if we let him guide us, we will find rest for our souls? Is he saying that his "yoke" (his rule? his demands upon our lives?) is easier to carry than the baggage we're lugging on our own?

Try it out and see. Put your empty bag or backpack on the floor at your feet. Then pick up one of the rocks or weights and ask God what burden it represents. Name the rock. What is it? A duty? A specific guilt? A person you're feeling too responsible for? A job you dread? Fear about money? Once you know its name, put it in the bag. Now pick up another rock. Ask it *its* name! Put the second weight in the bag. Keep going until you've named all your burdens or you've reached your bench press limit!

Now pick up your bag, sling it on your back and start walking through the house, around the room, up and down stairs, feeling the weight of your burdens. Do you want help? Do you want to keep carrying the bag? What's keeping you from handing the bag to Jesus? Think about it. Are you ready to give it to him? Imagine Jesus standing somewhere in the room. Look at him. When you're ready, walk over and lay your burdens at Jesus' feet. Ask him if he'll take care of them. Say whatever you want to say to him. What is he saying to you?

Notes, drawings, insights, thoughts:

Prayer: Jesus—I know I don't see you clearly enough, but help me to trust that you're there. Help me to hand you the weights I am carrying. This is what they are, Jesus, I'll name them for you:_____

_____. Here they are. Will you carry them? Thank you. Amen.

Praying for Others

Scripture: **Exodus 32:11–14; Ephesians 3:14–19**

Supplies: A newspaper, news magazine, or go to your Internet news source

Read the Exodus passage. Years after seeing God in the burning bush, Moses prays for the Jewish people. The people *loved* the beginning of the trip, when they left Egypt, but at this point they were getting a little cranky. Moses heard a lot whining from the back seat about "Are we *there* yet?" They decided they'd ignore the real God and create their own more manageable version. They made a little gold "god" statue in the shape of a calf. God was furious and threatened to wipe them out. Moses prayed and reminded God of God's promise to bring these rebellious, short-sighted people out of Egypt, and of an old promise God had made to Abraham and Sarah. Moses prayed like a lawyer arguing a case, using precedents. God changed his mind.

Paul intercedes for the people in the Ephesian church. He asks God to give the Ephesians the blessings God already wants them to have. (It's a softer, kinder version than the Moses prayer!) How do human beings have the audacity to *ask* God for anything, let alone almost *argue* with God, as Moses did? Remember that God has asked us to pray about the smallest things in our lives. (Remember the Lord's Prayer?) Somehow, our prayers matter to God. *We* matter to God.

So pick up your local paper, a news magazine, or go to an Internet news source. First, pray that God will show you who or what to pray for. Then leaf through the pages or scan the links. Something will catch your eye—a picture of a child in Afghanistan, an old man in the Bronx, a story of an epidemic or a war, an educational or environmental issue.

Sit quietly and breathe deeply. Ask God to use you to pray for this situation. Ask Jesus to show you his own feelings for these people—his compassion, his love, his pain. You could envision holding these people, or town or situation, or country in your hands. Focus on God using your hands to hold and bless these people. Ask God to have compassion, or heal, or to give them whatever insight or care they need. If people have been stupid, ask God to forgive them. You may not know what they need, but God does. When the prayer is done, thank God and say "Amen."

Notes, drawings, thoughts:

Prayer: O Holy God, you have told us that you created us, love us and will protect us and all people. I know you're telling the truth. Please care for these people / this situation. Heal it, or fix it, or fill it with your love and power. We are all in your hands. Jesus asked us to pray. Please use my prayers. Amen.

Just *Talk* with Your Prayer Partner!

You're great! Congratulations! What an intense week of prayer you've finished. How has this week been? Would you like a day to relax a bit? Meet with your prayer partner and talk about everything. How did this week affect you? Which prayer exercise did you like best? Which one was hardest, or which did you like least? What did you learn? What was hard? What do you wonder about? Did you get any different sense of God? Explain.

Talk about what's going on in each of your lives. How can your prayer partner focus his/her prayer while praying for you during this coming week?

Pray for each other together now, and for the people and situations you've become aware of this week. Be sure to pray for your partner specifically this week.

Notes, insights, lists, thoughts:

Reflection Day

Read. Read chapter 3 to prepare for your Experiment Group meeting tomorrow.

Review. Think back over your week of prayer. Review your notes, lists, insights. How is your prayer going? Review *Using Your Prayer Journal*, page 123. Ask God which ideas you need to pay attention to this week. Take some notes.

Answer two questions:

Question 1: What are the most important things you've learned/discovered/remembered this week?

Question 2: What do you wonder about?

Prayer: Talk to God. Sit in silence for a bit. Listen. Amen.

Courage. Transparency. Joy.

I committed to pray 30 minutes a day for this Unbinding coaching process. It almost killed me at the beginning! I was embarrassed to have to face the fact that I've never prayed much. Here I am a pastor, and I've never really prayed.

It took a lot of guts on my part to admit this out loud, but I asked a couple of men in my church to hold me accountable. They said they'd pray for me. That really embarrassed me—it never occurred to me to ask them to pray for me. If I'd thought about it, it might have felt presumptuous. But to be honest, it just never occurred to me. So we're trying an experiment. We're praying. We're meeting once a week for breakfast. I know they'll ask if I'm actually praying, so I'm praying my 30 minutes every day. It's still hard, but it's getting easier.

Meetings are less tense at church. I'm able to listen better. Two things are happening in the church. Ministry is fun in a way I've never experienced in 20 years. And the church (and I) are getting creative. People are coming up with great ideas for things to do with kids, and worship and a couple of projects to help the neighborhood around the church. It has never been this fun before. We're all scratching our heads.

My wife says it would be a good thing if I kept this up.

—Anonymous!

CHAPTER 3

It's a Marathon—Not a Sprint

My brother Gil called me on my birthday last year.

"Hey!" Gil said. "Happy birthday!....Oh my gosh! There's this book you've got to read—*Younger Next Year.*"[1]

"!!!! **Gil!** That is **_so rude!_** Did you even **get** me a copy, or are you just mentioning this to help me embrace a new year?"

He referred me to Amazon.com, then gave me a 20-minute riff on the book. You probably need to hear it, too, so I'll summarize for you:

Many of us are going to live **very** long lives because American medical care is so advanced. Most of us face an important choice. We can live well into our 80's and feel horrible, creaky and cranky, slugging down more and more Aleve.™ **Or** we can live well into our 80's and beyond, and feel **great** pretty much right up until the end.

If we will work out hard enough to break a sweat **six** days a week and lift weights **two** of those days, we have a good shot at having a healthy 50-year-old body for as long as we live. If we work out, we statistically decrease our chances of getting 70 percent of the diseases and accidents of old age.

"What???" Lift weights?? Oh, yeah. **Sure**. I am like so **totally** going to lift **weights**, Gil. Right!"

Well, I'm doing it. It takes discipline, but it's getting more normal, and much more fun. A tiny, little 5' 2" trainer at the YMCA taught me how to do the weight machines. I imagined the only people inside gyms were muscle-bound troglodytes, striding about the room with six-packs (the buff kind **and** the Budweiser kind), flexing biceps covered with those wormy, sticking-out veins.

"The exercises have helped greatly. I love the 'doing' ones! I've also realized how spiritually thirsty I was and have started a practice of spending one day a month praying, to simply spend time with God. I feel like a wilting plant that is now coming back to life."

—*an eastern judicatory minister (like a bishop)*

33

Well, Arnold Schwarzenegger doesn't **go** to my Y, although you do run into the occasional retired Marine who inspires respect. I asked the lady doing the triceps machine how long she'd been lifting weights. "Since I had my hip replaced three years ago. I've kept doing it because I feel great and I do **not** want to get like my mother when she got old. She made herself and all the rest of us miserable. I'm not that old yet, though. I'm only 78." Totally inspiring 80-year-olds, a man with cerebral palsy, a woman who was in a bad car accident, and courageous people who weigh 325 pounds go to **my** Y.

The Training Effect & The Zone

Okay, here's the deal. A spiritual life is a lot like a physical life. It thrives with practice, discipline, accountability and actually doing it. It gets to be a lot of fun, and it makes you feel great. I don't think it's an accident that people call different types of prayer and ways of relating to God "spiritual **exercises**." Over the millennia, people have figured out what works best to help us develop a healthy spiritual life.

Most churches don't pray much. We pray in worship (well, the **pastor** prays during worship, and people bow their heads). I realized years ago that we only let ourselves pray for a church member when they're sick. In most churches, you don't **want** to be sick enough to get prayed for. I know this isn't ever a conscious, or articulated thought, but I think most church people presume that prayer is something elderly ladies do, or Catholic monks do, or atheists in foxholes do, or sweet, sentimental, nice people do. It doesn't seem like the purview of veterinarians, restaurant workers, lawyers, or truck drivers.

This is a mistake. It's a **big** mistake.

I am a lawyer as well as a pastor. I'm not sweet. I have moments of compassion and kindness, but they're a gift of the Holy Spirit, brought about by decades of prayer. Here's what I've learned about prayer: it's for athletes. It's for the strongest, toughest leaders. It's for the kindest, gentlest spirits. Trying to live a courageous, faithful life without prayer is like heading up Mount Everest without belaying ropes and anchoring systems. Prayer is our lifeline to God. Through it, God provides our guidance, our safety and our power. Prayer isn't sentimental.

I can describe prayer as I have experienced it. Prayer feels like training to me. It feels like swim team, marathon, or language training. You learn skills, the vocabulary, the basic rules and parameters. You train for an interminable amount of time. You get better at it. (The training effect) THEN, after time, you experience the high of being in the Zone!

We only understand miniscule bits of the majesty, power and love of the infinite God. We live in a world that God is saturating with holy presence. We just haven't learned to see it, or we're too used to it, or we skim by it as we race on to the next thing in our lives.

I like distance sports best. I loved running before I trashed a knee. Marathon training takes ages. You train, with a fairly compulsive schedule. Your body adapts slowly to increasing mileage, with occasional speed play. After months and years of training, you can experience long stretches of time during long runs (never at the beginning, usually after miles) when you feel as if you could run, floating like a leaf on the breeze, forever. It's effortless. It's absolute joy.

That's what prayer's like, at least for me. My heart doesn't naturally leap with joy at the thought of praying every morning. I just do it. After years of trying different things, I have more and more moments of feeling in the Zone—that God is there, with me, with numinous moments of a sense of presence. That's wonderful. There's a training effect with prayer. I love being in the Zone with the Spirit, but even if that never happened, the training effect is worth it.

No matter how the prayer "feels," if I pray, I'm generally more responsive to God. I tend to have more moments of being really usable by the Spirit. And my life is usually way more fun, and almost always much more real.

So, I commend it to you.

> "The session (the church board) is now taking notes on how to pray for one another. We're putting the prayer up on our refrigerators so we can pray for each other every day."

What Does Spiritual Training Look Like?

1. We do it with friends. You cannot live a spiritual life in isolation. We do it with buddies. That's basically what churches are—or should be—collection grounds for people who want to keep learning, who want to see God more clearly, to love God more, to live more powerfully and help other people. We don't have to pray or figure out life from the bottom of an isolation tank. We work together. We help each other.

2. We do it alone—with God. Each one of us can be a tiny part of the whole church. The church is a collection of billions of Christians that stretches thousands of years through time. Each of us is born, lives a unique life and dies. We live with other people, and we can choose to live in the context of a loving community, but even twins live separate lives. We can never live in lockstep forever with another person. The only one with whom we can spend our whole life, every minute, inseparably, is God. Each of us can choose to offer our soul and our lives to God, day after day. Prayer is the one-by-one way we communicate with God. God breathes infinity into us through prayer.

3. A spiritual life involves our whole selves—mind, body, work, play, sex, credit card and school debt, politics, eating, money, communities, families, nations—every area of our lives. Nothing's left outside. The spiritual life affects everything: all thoughts, all actions, all relationships.

4. A spiritual life stagnates if we stop. You can't hoard spiritual wisdom—a relationship with God is more like a running stream than a dammed up lake. Woody Allen said to Diane Keaton in Annie Hall, "Relationships are a lot like sharks. If they stop moving, they die."[2] We need to keep moving, learning, praying, serving. Every day.

5. What can we rely on to learn more about God? The Bible; wisdom the church has learned over the ages; our unique life experiences (including our prayer lives and what we see in other people's lives); and rigorous, logical thinking.

"Never, never, never, never give in."[3]

—Winston Churchill

6. Key elements of a spiritual life? Love God, study scripture, be accountable to mature people, worship God in a group, and keep praying. Let God use us to serve some of the other people God loves.

7. You'll experience "dry" times. You could experience a stretch of time—if you're sick, if you're in grief—when your prayer could feel "flat," as if God has moved far away. Some of the most mature Christians feel as if they're doing something wrong if this happens. Don't blame yourself. Don't stop. This is normal. This is why a group of friends and a prayer partner are so important. When we're thrown for a loop and God seems to disappear, Christ may actually appear to us "through" our friends.

8. Spiritually stronger next year? Pray six out of seven days. Do the heavy lifting. I'll let you unpack that yourself, but basically, spiritual growth is just like physical growth. The people who are really fit work out every day, hard enough to break a sweat. Just do something every day. Weekend warriors don't run marathons. A spiritual life is a marathon.

9. We'll always be fragile, limited, messed-up people! AND God can help us mature. God can do amazing things for other people through us. Human potential, working with God, is staggering. If we will spend our lives trying to learn how much God loves us, and trying to love God, God promises to help us become more like Christ.

Types of Prayer

Let's talk about different types of prayer. You've already done quite a few of them in the daily prayer exercises. Basically, prayer is all part of a huge, lifelong, off-and-on conversation with God. **God communicates with us**—through Scripture, through other people, through events in our lives (okay, we talked about that last week), through our thinking and studying and realizations and maturing as spiritual people, and in a lifetime of learning to be silent and listen. <u>**We communicate with God**</u> in all sorts of ways—we can express to God every emotion we experience in our relationships with people.

You know how human relationships deepen and develop over time? The first year of a great marriage isn't the same as it is 50 years later. Newlyweds gaze besottedly at each other, burst into tears, escape to the bar with their friends and have a **lot** of fun making up after the fight. They're madly in love.

Fifty years later, the couple loves each other dearly, but there's not a lot that's going to surprise them about each other. They get quieter. They can sit together for hours, communication open, no words needed. Our relationship with God is the same way. It deepens and develops over time. It gets quieter. If we keep growing with God, the layers and lines of communication between us deepen. A sideways glimpse and a shared smile suffice. We need fewer words.

Sister Anna was a friend and a Benedictine sister. She prayed consistently for 70 of her 82 years. Her spiritual director asked her to pray through Isaiah, chapters 40 through 45 during one of her last week-long silence retreats. She started at Chapter 40, verse 1. By the end of the week, she had reached Chapter 40, verse 31. It wasn't that she was old and falling asleep with tedium. No. God overwhelmed her with love and a sense of profound truth. The words were so richly layered after a lifetime of hearing them, studying them, living them that she fell into a well of meaning as she read each phrase. She explained, "there's so much **there**. I couldn't rush past everything the Lord was showing me."

A life of faith isn't a sprint. It's a marathon. Marathons are built on slow, steady, daily training. It's not likely that we'll slip one day and fall into being a spiritually luminous 80-year-old. Numinous octogenarians emerge from a long, divine-human building process.

Our part is to be available to God as well as we can. Don't worry. We won't do it very well. Our best efforts usually have a "sorta, kinda, oh, wow I forgot" quality to them. The good news is that if we'll even try to show up, God can work with us. God can work miracles with that.

What kind of prayer will help us mature in our spiritual relationship with God, with Christ, with the Spirit? Hundreds of ways of praying exist. Some are very old. You've already experimented with quite a few during the past two weeks. The main point is just to talk with God about the things in your life. Expand your life by study and prayer. Then talk to God and listen to God about the new things you're learning and living! If you were to divide life into types of things you're living and learning, you could divide up the kinds of prayer that go with those aspects of your life. Here are some types of prayer that I can think of off the top of my head:

"Prayer is a new concept. I thought I had to be holy to pray. Now I pray when I'm working out on exercise machines, at the coffee shop and on my walk. I'm having fun."

- **Praise of God** ("Oh, Holy One! I praise you for even the little I understand of you!")

- **Thanksgiving** ("Look at what you've done! Look at who you are! Thank you!")

- **Sacred reading / Praying with scripture** ("Lectio divina," pronounced "LEX-ee-o diVIna," We are praying using lectio the first day of most weeks.)

- **Examination**, or "examen" (What have I done wrong or right? Christ, help me look back over the day with your eyes. Help me learn and be more like you.)

- **Meditational prayers** (e.g., the Jesus Prayer, see Week D, Day 3)

- **Confession** ("I did it." "I'm sorry, friend." "I'm sorry, God." See some of the Day 2 prayers.)

- **"Slice of life" prayers** (Prayers at stoplights, when an ambulance goes by, praying instantaneously for someone who flashes through your mind)

- **Discernment** (Try to see a situation with Christ's eyes, or to figure out what God would like us to do.)

- **Reconciliation** ("Please, God, help this person and me get over our disagreement or estrangement")

- **Lament prayers** (God, how long must I endure this? Do whatever you have to — please get me out of this situation.)

- **Desert prayers** (Sit in emptiness with God when you are numb from a great loss, or because of the beauty of the emptiness.)

- **Intercession** (Pray for others)

- **Healing** (Ask God for healing for illnesses, painful things in our pasts, for relationships, really any kind of healing.)

- **A Moses arguing/Job prayer** (God—I'm hurt! I'm furious. I feel betrayed by people and by YOU. This isn't fair!!! I don't understand. Will you fix it? Will you be with me, even if I don't understand? I will try to trust. Please help me.)

- **Silent prayer** (Sit quietly. Let go of your thoughts and feelings to just be with God.)

- **Prayers with others** (You've been doing this each week with your group.)

- **Liturgy** (Formal, spoken prayer in worship services)

- **Worship** with other Christians is also prayer.

See? Prayer matches any situation, any time in your life, any mood, any stage of growth. Don't let this list overwhelm you. It just points to various natural moments in your life that can turn into moments of meditation and prayer. Each day let a bit of prayer match your mood. Pray or talk with friends about faith issues. Read something in the Bible. Go to a class. Sit on a park bench and try to listen to God. Repeat a phrase you like from the Bible while you run on the treadmill. Worship with a community of people. We get the most benefit, over time, from small, steady, daily doses. It's just like physical exercise.

St. Paul told the people in the church in Rome something crucially important: "…the Spirit helps us in our weakness; for we do not know how to pray as we ought, but that very Spirit intercedes with sighs too deep for words" (Romans 8:26). Here's my best, quick understanding of what Paul's saying: We don't need to know everything. We don't have to be perfect. All we need is to be willing, and God can use us. The Spirit is the living, breathing, active presence of God and of Christ. The Spirit's with us all the time and ready to help us navigate through our lives. The Spirit will "pray through us" in ways we can't understand.

Our part is to be available to God as well as we can. Don't worry. We won't do it very well! Our best efforts usually have a "sorta, kinda, oh, wow I forgot" quality to them. Going face-to-Face with God scares us as much as the burning bush terrified Moses. The good news is that if we'll even *try* to show up, God can work with us. God can work *miracles* with that. Our part in this divine-human conversation is pretty humble. Yet it's the greatest conversation in the world. All we have to do is to keep talking and listening.

Every day.

Prayer is for athletes. It's for the strongest, toughest leaders. It's for the kindest, gentlest spirits. Trying to live a courageous, faithful life without prayer is like heading up Mount Everest without belaying ropes and anchoring systems. Prayer is our lifeline to God. Through it, God provides our guidance, our safety and our power. Prayer isn't sentimental.

[1]Chris Crowley & Henry S. Lodge, *Younger Next Year* (and *Younger Next Year for Women*) (New York: Workman Publishing Company, 2007).
[2]*Annie Hall*, MGM, 1977.
[3]Winston Churchill, British Prime Minister, in a speech given at Harrow School on October 29, 1941.

GROUP DISCUSSION_____

1. How has your prayer gone this week? What has made you break a sweat? What gets your spiritual heart rate up? What's a challenge? What's great?

2. You started this process two weeks ago. What have you learned? Has God surprised you? How do you feel about the group, the people? How is your prayer life going? Have you surprised yourself?

3. Have you experienced any personal relationship or encounter with God?

4. Discuss what you think about the ideas in chapter 3. What do you wonder about?

5. Did you interview someone? What did you discover?

GROUP EXERCISE *(take about half your group time to do this)* _____

Divide into groups of three. Sit quietly for about a minute and think, or if you can, ask God:

"What's the most important thing I'm learning in this process?" (Your facilitator will tell you when the time is up). *Jot down some notes:*

Now close your eyes for another minute or two and ask yourself (and God):

"What more can I learn/ask/discover/get from this group?"

Notes:

> Our part in this divine-human conversation is pretty humble. Yet it's the greatest conversation in the world. All we have to do is to keep talking and listening. Every day. We don't need to know everything. We don't have to be perfect. All we need is to be willing, and God can use us.

Talk, then pray. Take a minute or two to tell the group what you experienced when you asked these questions. Pray silently for each person as they speak. When everyone has shared, pray for each person, using Prayer Triads.

PRAYER TRIADS *(Praying for Each Other)* _____

Divide into small groups of three. The leader will keep time. First, sit in silent prayer for two minutes. Breathe deeply, exhale and relax. Ask God to let you know the one thing you should ask these two people to pray about for you. It could be anything—to know God better, forgiveness, strength to face a specific situation, healing of anger, growth in patience or love, understanding of some confusing relationship or situation, strength to deal with an addiction. Who knows? Ask God!

There's only one rule: the prayer must be for *you*—not your mother or your child or people at work! Ask God what *you* need prayer for. After the leader rings the bell to signal the end of your minute of silence, tell the others how they can focus their prayer for you in one short, timed minute. (Your leader will ring a bell or signal you at the end of each person's "This is how you can focus your prayer for me" minute.)

As soon as you have each taken your minute to share your prayer requests, pray for each other. You may use spoken or silent prayer. You may wish to lay a hand gently on the arm or shoulder of the person for whom you are praying. Take no longer than six minutes total to pray for all three of you.

(Facilitators — discuss in advance different ways of praying with and for others. Let groups decide how they'll pray together. Divide the prayer time evenly and let everyone know when it's time to start praying for the next person so that everyone will be prayed for. (Otherwise, we extroverts will grab the time and never get prayed for!)

Community. You are studying, praying with scripture, already doing many of the types of spiritual disciplines we described in this chapter. You may want to add one more discipline to the prayer, study and discussion - worship. You might think of all attending worship together this Sunday, then going out to lunch together.

Close with the Lord's Prayer.

A life of faith isn't a sprint. It's a marathon. Marathons are built on slow, steady, daily training.

Be Strong and Courageous

God Is with You Wherever You Go

Scripture: Joshua 1:1–9

Light your candle and get calm. Exhale. Offer God this time and yourself. Now read the beginning of the book of Joshua. Moses led the people in the wilderness for 40 years, for a generation. He died, and the people were still wandering in the desert. Joshua would lead them next. Imagine how you'd feel in Joshua's place as you read these words.

Read the passage again slowly. Which phrases seem most important? Write them down. Sit silently for a few minutes. Ask God to show you whatever else you need to see in the passage. Read it out loud to yourself. Sit. Listen to anything the passage may be saying that applies to your life. What does God want you to hear in these words?

Take a 3 x 5 card and write down the sentence that feels most important. Carry it in your pocket today. Look at it and repeat it out loud to yourself at least 10 times today. Memorize the words. When the day is done, write the words here, from memory.

Notes, drawings, thoughts, insights:

Prayer: Say the words of your sentence from Joshua 1 as a prayer. Sit for a minute and ask God to show you very clearly what you have learned from that sentence. Say the words out loud, again as a prayer. Amen.

Are You a Worrier?

Scripture: Matthew 6:25–34; 1 Peter 5:6–7

Sit quietly for a minute and ask God to be with you as you give God this time. Take a deep breath and exhale slowly. Now read the text from Matthew's Gospel. Will you read it again, slowly?

Did you tense up?

Are you a worrier? I am. I wake up at 2 in the morning sometimes, stewing about stuff. I twist everything out of proportion in the middle of the night. There's this totally unredeemed part of me that just **knows** that I can handle situations better than anyone else, and probably better than God, who I forget about. Oh, I **wish** I were a better person, but that's the truth if I'm honest with myself. When someone, even Jesus, tells me "Don't worry," it doesn't help me that much. I'm not **choosing** to worry—I just automatically **go** there!

What can we do? We can realize, over time, that God exists and that God will care for us in specific, providential ways. The more real my relationship with God gets, the more I know that if I let go of my stranglehold on situations (even if it's a secret, spiritual stranglehold), God has more leeway to work with me. Let go. Hand it over. Leave it to God.

Close your eyes and ask God what you're worrying about right now. Let the worries float up out of your gut, into your conscious mind. Write them down here, in words, images, drawings, or symbols, as they emerge. Now, ask God which ones you're **most** worried about. Number them in order of how much they get to you! Look at the list. Think, one by one, "I'm giving this worry to you, Lord." Now close the book and hold it, praying for any people involved and asking for faith to leave all these situations in God's hands for the day.

Notes, drawings, thoughts:

Insight: "At night, I give my troubles to God. He's going to be up all night anyway."
Calligraphy on a notecard from Sister Cornelia Gust, Order of St. Benedict,
Crookston, Minnesota

Prayer: Oh, Holy One! I'm a mess, and I'm a worrier! Please help me see, in one specific situation today, that you really are here and will care for me. Amen.

Your Whole-Self Prayer

Scripture: 1 Corinthians 6:19–20

We tend to think of our emotions, and mind, and soul, and body as separate things. We pray, but in our heads, our prayer isn't connected with our work. We exercise, but don't think of that as connected with whether we're feeling affectionate toward our families. Well, it's all connected. Modern science and spiritual teaching for thousands of years agree. St. Paul tells us that our bodies are temples for the Holy Spirit. We can grow in our spiritual lives if we help God "connect the dots" between our minds and our bodies and our spirits. Let's try to connect prayer and exercise today.

One thing prayer does is to help us detach from all of the daily lists, duties, harassments, habits and addictions. Exercise does the same thing. Exercise can be a time for prayer. Exercise can **become** prayer. So let's try a literal prayer exercise today. Marathoners, cane-walkers, swimmers, dancers, weight lifters, wheelchair athletes, basketball players—pick your sport!

Go to your exercise place. Drink some water. Ask God to help you let go of the disappointments, worries, sins that have collected inside you. Then start moving slowly. Ask God to bless the exercise and to turn it into prayer. As you move, think about your breath. Breathe in and feel as if you're breathing in new air that will expand you, clear you out, and give you holy inspiration. ("Inspiration" comes from a Greek word that means "to breathe in.") Exhale and imagine the old ideas, obsessive thinking, stale opinions, frustrations moving out of your body and soul.

After a while, pick up the pace to fit what your body needs. Inhale—ask the Spirit of Christ to come into you and to heal you. Exhale and let go of more internal clutter! You could repeat a prayer, or a short scripture phrase, over and over, in time with your breathing. Here are a couple of suggestions:

"[Inhale] Those who wait for the Lord [exhale] shall renew their strength."
(Isaiah 40:31), *OR*

"[Inhale] The Lord my God is with me, [exhale] wherever I go."
(like Joshua 1:9 - remember Monday?)

Notes, lists, drawings, ideas:

Prayer: Oh God, let my body be a holy temple for your Holy Spirit. Will you help me be more aware of you today? Will you give me a couple of moments when I'm really aware of you, or your kindness to me? Amen.

Far Away

Scripture: Luke 15:11–24

Light your candle. Get calm. Release the tension in your jaw and shoulders. Today is a prayer day for other people. Let's start with the person. Do you love someone, or are you concerned about someone who seems "lost?" …"gone" in some way? We can lose people—or feel lost ourselves—through arguments, physical or mental illness, broken relationships, substance abuse, accidents, or violence. They can be sitting across the table from you, but still "gone." Close your eyes and ask God if there's someone "lost to you" for whom you could pray.

Now read this story. It's sometimes called the story of the "prodigal son." Jesus tells the story to describe what God's like. See how the son was lost? He basically told his father he wished the father were dead ("give me my share of the property I'll inherit when you die," verse 12), grabbed the money, squandered it (verse 13), and was starving among strangers (verses 14-15).

Can you imagine what the father felt as he wondered about his absent son? Have you ever felt like a lost, angry boy? Look what happens when the son was brave enough to go home. Instead of slamming the door in the boy's face, the father welcomes him in and gives him a party. God thinks about all of us this way.

We can pray for people who are absent, even if they seem unreachable right now. You might pull out a photo of the person when they were whole or happy. Somewhere, that healthy child or great dad still lives inside the person who is "gone." (If the person has a mystery face—like an unknown birth mom—take a blank piece of paper, and let it represent them.) Look at the picture. Pray that God can heal the present person through that little bit of them that's still the person in the picture. Or visualize the person's most loving, best quality, even though it's submerged now. Sit quietly, imagine that you're holding that healthy part of them in your hands, and offer that health to God to "grow." Ask God to heal the person you love and miss, no matter what that healing looks like. We can't make anyone else's choices for them, but we *can* pray.

Notes, insights, drawings, thoughts:

Prayer: Oh, God, I know we're all lost and wandering. I have forgotten you and run away from you so many times. Please take me back. And I ask, in your mercy, that you care for, and love, and heal—in whatever way is best—my beloved _____.
Help them, and help me rest in you and not expect the outcome I want. Amen.

A Prayer Walk with Your Partner

Scripture: James 5:13–18; Romans 8:26–27

Preparation: *Read this ahead of time, and talk by phone with your partner. Decide where you're going to meet to pray.*

When you get together, talk about how your prayer has gone this week. What has happened? What are you thinking about? What drove you crazy? What did you love? Did you change your mind or heart about anything? Did any insights burst upon you? What meaning and purpose do you see in what you are doing?

Go somewhere public with your prayer partner. Pick a neighborhood, or a sit on a couple of benches at a park, or the mall. Then think about the fact that God is right there. In your head, ask Jesus to let you see the people around you with his eyes. Ask God's Spirit to "pray through you," even if you don't know exactly how to pray. (See Romans 8:26. The Spirit will actually do the praying through us when we don't know how to pray.) Which people around you do you notice? Can you imagine what that man's life is like? Pray for him. Pray that God will bless that woman and give her whatever she really needs. Pray for kids on roller blades. Bless the physical place you're in. Ask that it be filled with God and be filled with joy. Ask that the neighbors watch out for each other.

You might take a "prayer walk" through a neighborhood. Walk slowly, and pray for each house as you pass it, the families and visitors, moving cars and parked cars. Touch a stop sign and pray that people will see it! One of you may pray for the right side of the street, the other for the left. Walk quietly together, and "think" your prayer to God. Ask Jesus to walk through the neighborhood with you. (He is already doing it, but asking may help us realize it!) Pray for God's presence, peace and protection to blanket the area. Pray that the neighborhood be infused with Christ's presence.

How did you experience the time and the prayer?

Notes, drawings, thoughts:

Reflection Day

Read. Read chapter 4 in preparation for your group's meeting tomorrow.

Review. Think back over your week of prayer. Reread your favorite scripture from the week. Review your notes, lists, insights. How is your prayer going?

Then, answer two questions:

Question 1: What are the most important things you've learned/discovered/remembered this week?

Question 2: What do you wonder about?

Prayer: Talk to God. Sit in silence for a bit. Listen. Amen.

Do it now!

Watch Susan Boyle, 47 years old, unemployed, frumpy,
never-been-kissed, Scottish church worker,
who lives with her cat Pebbles,
amaze the audience, the judges and the world
as she sings "I Dreamed a Dream" in the
Britain's Got Talent *competition:*

www.youtube.com
Enter "Susan Boyle Britains Got Talent 2009"
in the search box.

(If you don't have a computer, go visit a friend,
the office, or the library!

You'll LOVE this!)

CHAPTER 4

Step Over the Line

I'm no expert on children, but I *was* a child and I've watched a lot of children. Brothers punch each other. Sisters draw invisible lines down the middles of bedrooms, under dining room tables, and on couches in front of the TV. I remember car trips to Florida where back-seat negotiations resembled emergency sessions of the United Nations' Security Council.

"Hey! You're in my space! Get over."

"You're not the boss of me!"

"*Here's* the line. Everything on this side of it is *MY* side. You stay on *YOUR* side. That's all *your* space over *there*. Just don't cross over onto *my* side, or you are going to be in *So Much Trouble.*"

We drew lines with each other. We drew lines in the sand when we played with the Kennedy and the Van Voorhis kids. Our parents drew lines. In that case, we were absolutely certain that they *were* the boss of us.

The more I think about it, my life is full of lines. I know what's on *my* side of the line. Once I step over it, I'm in unknown territory—on someone else's turf. It might be fun. It might be dangerous. One thing's clear: once I step over the line, I'm on someone else's ground. I'm not in control.

I tend to stay on my side.

Let's shift gears. Søren Kierkegaard, a brilliant, Danish, Lutheran philosopher and theologian, lived in the early 1800's. He believed that learning, hard work and "knowing" things is the way to flourish in most areas of our lives. But just *knowing* stuff and working hard

Over and over, no matter how we feel, we need to let God do whatever God wants to do with us. Heal us, or not. Use us, or not. Give us the dream we have for our lives, or not. Help us forgive that person, or not. Catch us when we fall, or not. Give us a new life, or not. Allow us to serve God, to work with God, to live with God into eternity, one step at a time, or not. *Then* God can work with us!

**doesn't** work with our spiritual lives. We can study the Bible and read theology all our lives, but if we don't take a "leap to faith" (agree to surrender control of our lives), if we don't cross over into God's part of the "room," we'll never understand who God is or what our lives can be.

We can amass spiritual and religious information, but until we take the step off that cliff, we'll never know that God will catch us. The beginning of a real spiritual life, according to Kierkegaard, is when we take the terrifying step to trust God rather than our own efforts to keep ourselves safe.[1]

If someone wants to do a "show and tell" for your group meeting this week, show the scene from _Butch Cassidy and the Sundance Kid_[2] where the lawmen have tracked and chased Butch and Sundance for days. The lawmen corner the heroes (bank robbers) on a rock outcropping high above a roaring, boulder-filled river. Two options remain: they jump into the river, or they get caught. They decide to jump. Robert Redford, Mr. Blasé, shows his first visible emotion: fear.

"I can't swim."

Paul Newman, slowly grins his twinkly-blue-eyed smile, and laughs, "You can't _**swim**_??? The _**fall's**_ gonna kill ya."

That's the feel of a leap to faith.

I think that's what Kierkegaard was talking about. We have to take a leap _**of**_ faith, a leap _**to**_ faith. But God is so powerful and mysterious that even though it feels as if _**we're**_ scraping together the courage to jump, it's actually God all the time. God calls us to trust and jump. God gives us the courage. God helps us make the leap. God catches us.

We need to let God invite us to jump into God's arms—however you envision crossing over onto God's turf. We need to jump over and over as people of faith. Wow! Jumping is counterintuitive, after a lifetime of learning _**not**_ to leave the carefully negotiated safety zone that's _**my**_ third of the back seat of the car.

We learn self-reliance well. Yet critical points loom up in a life of faith when we need to hand the controls to God. If you pin really mature Christians to the wall, they'll tell you that they've endured many episodes of deciding to trust God in situations that seem hopeless. One 65-year-old man told me, "It's HORRIBLE! Every time I'm on some new 'edge' with God, every time God's trying to teach me the next thing or move me in some new direction, I seize up. I feel

Self-relinquishment lies at the heart of faith. The idea of "handing ourselves" to God, of "surrendering," or "yielding," or saying "yes," or taking a leap to faith appears throughout the Bible. This self-relinquishment makes it possible to accept the new, true self that God can place in our now-empty hands.

as if I need to run a couple of laps to get rid of the tension. It always feels as if I'm giving up the one idea or the one chunk of money, or the one bit of leisure time that's keeping my life in control."

Then you hand it to God and it turns out to be okay.

Over and over, no matter how we *feel*, we need to let God do whatever God wants to do with us. Use us, or not. Give us the dream we have for our lives, or not. Help us forgive that person, or not. Catch us when we fall, or not. Give us a new life, or not. Allow us to serve God, to work with God, to live with God into eternity, one step at a time, or not. *Then* God can work with us!

Jesus embodied this key dynamic of faith. He surrendered everything, including his life, to God. He was arrested one night. Just before the arrest, he prayed. He knew what was coming and asked God to save him. Jesus finished praying by saying that if God needed him to die (trust/jump), he'd do it. Jesus prayed for courage.

> "I'm trying to develop a risk-taking spirit. I want to be willing to let this thing happen even if I have doubts about it."
>
> *– a Westerner*

The political officials and the people killed him the next day. He died a brutal death. Three days later, God brought him back to life and in the next weeks, hundreds of people saw him, spoke with him, ate dinner with him. (You can read about it, starting at Matthew 26:36, going through the end of the book of Matthew, chapter 28.)

In some mysterious way, this type of self-relinquishment lies at the heart of faith. The idea of "handing ourselves" to God, of "surrendering," or "yielding," or saying "yes," or taking a leap to faith appears throughout the Bible.

It crops up in stories and teaching across thousands of years of Jewish and Christian history. This self-relinquishment makes it possible to accept the new, true self that God can place in our now-empty hands. It's possible in *our* lives.

> "I am now asking myself, "How much do I trust God?' I'm growing in my trust. God's not going to lead you into the desert and leave you there. I have a new confidence in God in my life."

Here's the main idea: God is God, and we're not. God's real. God loves us. Our lives can be powerful forces for good. God can fill our lives with joy, if we live each day in sync with this key reality. God is God. We're not God.

Wow. Is that ever counterintuitive for most of us! The good news is that God adores us and will let us help with great things that matter. We just need to take whatever next step of saying "yes" to God that God wants us to take.

What does your next step with God look like? I think we all need to ask God. Whoever we are—Stalin or Schweitzer; Manson or Mother Teresa, or any of us in between—we need to take the next step. We may have taken thousands of steps in faith before. *But the step that matters is the **next** step.* The questions tend to run along these lines:

"God, what's the next step? What am I using to hold you at arm's length? What can I hand you so that you can heal me, or make me stronger or more like Christ? What would you love for me to learn next? Do next? What's the next step? Will you help me take it? Help me to trust you, please!"

We all have responsibilities, broken dreams, ongoing struggles, joyous relationships, worries about parents and money, ruined relationships, fears for kids, anxieties, addictive patterns, illnesses and needs to have our lives *matter* in the world. Oh, the hopes that lurk in each one of us! …the bitterness we cling to! We have learned to trudge along, no matter how steep the path, staggering under the sheer tonnage of our burdens. But God will heal us, lift burdens from us, direct our steps and use us to help others, if we will step

> off our own turf,
> > over the line to faith,
> > > into God's territory.

Many people describe a specific moment when they took a step into faith. Sometimes a first step is a "yes" to the *idea* of God. Most serious Christians describe *many* moments of yieldedness in their spiritual lives. One moment or many, the quintessential movement of a Christian life is the moment of letting go of control, the moment of surrender, the moment of trust, the moment of obedience to the call to let go of our lives and entrust them to God. And God will even give us the trust, the faith, the obedience we need to obey.

God calls us to a surrender of self that is completely foreign to how we are naturally. Our normal way is to carve out our portion of the back seat as ours, as safe. God asks, over and over in our lives, if we'll cross over the safety line and venture into unknown, "un-owned" territory—onto God's turf. Until we do, we'll never know what courageous, exciting lives God can help us live.

The first Christians called each other brothers and sisters. It's all over the New Testament. Some churches say it today, "Christian brothers and sisters." It's the good side of the brother and sister relationship we're talking about in the church. Brothers and sisters may do a little arm punching at board meetings, but there's also a lot of protection and encouragement and love among the kids. And the kids grow up to be deeply loving, powerful adults who work humbly and miraculously with God.

"It was so scary to come to a church. It scared me to death to pray out loud with people. But I did it the third week. I can't believe how close my group is – we trust each other so much. We can say anything to each other. I love these people. I'm so glad God is letting me know Him and I get to be with my group."

Here's the main idea: God is God and we're not. God's real. God loves us. Our lives can be powerful forces for good. God can fill our lives with joy, if we live each day in sync with this key reality.

Christian brothers and sisters, at their best, cheer us on. They help us cross lines toward deeper faith in God. They point and say, "Look—there's a line. It's a chance to cross over to be with God. There's Christ, right over there, waiting for you. I know it's scary, but you can **do** it—go ahead. I'm praying for you right now. Go over there. Jump. He'll catch you."

---

[1]Søren Kierkegaard, *The Concept of Anxiety* (1844), reprint ed. Reidar Thomte (Princeton: Princeton University Press, 1980).

[2]*Butch Cassidy and the Sundance Kid*, 20th Century Fox, 1969.

[3] *(on this page, below)* Paul Gauche, Lutheran pastor extraordinaire, used an exercise similar to this with a youth group. The kids are 28 now and still remember "that day we stepped over the line."

God calls us to a surrender of self that is completely foreign to how we are naturally. Our normal way is to carve out our portion of the back seat as ours, as safe. God asks, over and over in our lives, if we'll cross over the safety line and venture into unknown, "un-owned" territory – onto God's turf. Until we do, we'll never know what courageous, exciting lives God can help us live.

GROUP DISCUSSION

1. Open with prayer.

2. How did your prayer go this week? What do you want to share with the group?

3. What about this chapter bothers you, or makes you wonder? Which ideas give you hope? Have you taken a leap to faith during the last three weeks? What was it like? Did you gain any clearer understanding of God? Of yourself?

GROUP EXERCISE[3]

Sit in silence for a few minutes. Ask God to show you if you could trust God more in some area of your life. Ask Jesus if there is any "line" he'd like you to cross to move into deeper faith. Is there any leap the Spirit would like to help you to take?

After you have prayed, stand up and move to places in the room with clear space in front of you. Stand quietly for a minute. If the Spirit showed you some area of your life in which God would like you to trust more or to surrender control, visualize a "line" somewhere in the room that symbolizes crossing over into trust in God. Focus on your invisible line. When you're ready, ask God to help you cross the line. Cross it.

Small Group Discussion

In groups of three, or as a whole group, share anything you'd like to about crossing your line. What happened? After you have talked, pray for each other using Prayer Triads (see page 41).

You cannot live a spiritual life in isolation. We do it with buddies. That's basically what churches are—or should be—collection grounds for people who want to keep learning, who want to see God more clearly, to love God more, to live more powerfully and help other people. We don't have to pray or figure out life from the bottom of an isolation tank. We work together. We help each other.

Dear Brothers and Sisters, you're done with your commitment to pray and talk about faith for four weeks. You've done amazing work, and I pray that God has blessed this time for you. If any of you choose to keep going as a group, you can move on to chapters 5 through 8, which contain four more group meetings and the other half of a set of 40 days of prayer.   Blessings, Martha Grace

Notes

Prepare for First Meeting—
Part Two
Reading Assignment

Read Introduction, chapter 5 & <u>Using Your Prayer Journal</u> (starting on page 123)
<u>before</u> your first group meeting.

Start Week D of your prayer journal the
day <u>after</u> your first group meeting.

When you finish chapter 8, you could invite friends to join you for
Part One—The Experiment in Prayer & Community.

Unbinding Your Soul

PART TWO | Faith & Courage

For I am convinced that neither death, nor life, nor angels, nor rulers, nor things present, nor things to come, nor powers, nor height, nor depth, nor anything else in all creation, will be able to separate us from the love of God in Christ Jesus our Lord.
(Romans 8:38-39)

The kids take hold

E-mail from a pastor of a large church that had prepared its leadership with small group studies of **Unbinding the Gospel** for eight months. Now the all-church saturation study with **Unbinding Your Heart** (the "E-vent") begins:

I was amazed at the way the 7th-11th graders responded. They were interested, active, and involved. Our fringe kids were the ones who jumped right in and took ownership of building an altar and prayer wall for the youth. They had such pride in what they accomplished for the group! These youth, who usually stay on the outside of things, were the first ones to grab hold and say, "YES!" to an experience that I know will bring us all closer.

During our closing time, the prayers that they posted on the wall weren't the "help me through my math test that I didn't study for" prayers. They were prayers for healed relationships, broken hearts, wholeness, and physical healing. I was floored! Again, this group has never shared like this before.

I truly believe it is because of two things: the growing momentum/ synergy of the E-vent and how it connects the entire church, as well as the many weeks of prayer for our church leading up to this. God is amazing and does wonderfully unimaginable things when we step back and let him!

CHAPTER 5

From Passengers to Riders

In the spring of 6th grade I felt like a grown-up for the first time. Grandmother Reese decided I was old enough to ride Cherokee, her horse. Cherokee lived with Grandmother's brother, Uncle Fleek. I'm not sure whether it was because of his close association with my relatives, or whether he was just like this naturally, but Cherokee was a *lot* like Grandmother *and* Uncle Fleek. He was brilliant, quirky, with a great sense of humor, and quite forceful. I was, like I said, 12.

Uncle Fleek gave me lessons. He taught me how to tag Black Angus calves' ears right after they're born in the field. This doesn't sound like riding, but it gives you a lot of practice hurling yourself onto the horse's back after the mother cows notice what's going on. Uncle Fleek also taught me how to do cavalry charges. Once I could barrel down the road at a dead run, waving my saber *(riding crop)* back and forth across Cherokee's neck, shouting army stuff like General Patton did when *he* was in 6th grade, Uncle Fleek decided I was ready to go out riding by myself. Cherokee took over the riding lessons from *that* point.

I decided where we went. We rode across farms and fields. We cantered beside streams. We could go seven miles out on country roads. I made all the decisions.

Actually, I made the decisions on the trip *out*.

Cherokee loved home. He liked hanging out with Traveler, Uncle Fleek's huge gray horse who was named for General Lee's Traveler. The instant Cherokee's head veered toward the barn, the 1200-pound horse ignored the 100-pound kid on his back, slipped the bits between his teeth and headed home. He headed home very, very

God is huge, infinite, through time, across the ages, and God cares for each of us in the tiniest details of our lives. That's true, and we're swimming in it! We live in the very midst of an awe-filled, overwhelmingly glorious, creative world, and the presence of God is all around us, knocking on the doors of our hearts.

59

quickly. I learned to hang on. But I soon accepted the inevitable—I was a passenger.

I'm an adult now. I look around at my friends. I look at myself. I see that a lot of us are passengers a lot of the time. It's not always a bad thing. We just ought to be aware of it.

We live only half awake. We do the same old things every day. I don't **decide** anything when I buy toothpaste. I reach for Crest™ paste with the silver, anti-tartar-formula triangle on the box. My car turns left out of the driveway to go to the store. I fold the laundry the same way every time. Actually, the laundry **did** change when my husband and I got married. We fold shirts the way **his** mom does and socks the way **my** mom does. It's stable now, though.

Think about church. Most of us go to church in our normal patterns (once a month, once a week, Christmas and Easter, five times a week, or never) because that's our habit. We sit in the same seat in the sanctuary, talk with the same friends, do the same kind of study, or don't go at all—because that's what we're used to. Life jolts us with so many tragedies, stresses, distractions, and challenges. Most of us are ready for some comfort food, some comfort church, some comfort hanging-out-at-home! Some days, it's good to have **anything** that's The Same. Here's a vote for *West Wing*[1] reruns and plain old Crest.™ We need stability!

Yep. We need stability, but we also need vivid life and change. We need to learn new things. We all know what happens when we don't exercise. We get a little chubby. We settle into the couch with that bag of chips. Backs creak. Joints ache. We need exercise for as long as we live—vigorous exercise, break-a-sweat, daily workouts.

I don't think it's an accident that they call prayer, fasting, journaling and tithing "spiritual exercises."

If we aren't involved in a changing, complicated community of people;
>   if we aren't learning new things all the time;
>>   if we aren't loving and serving other people in some tangible way;
>>>   if we aren't asking God every day to draw us close, to
>>>>   help us step over the line, to please **use** us,
then our spirits clot.

Wow, do I **not** want to turn into a crotchety grump. That's unpleasant for **everyone**.

"A friend in church told me she was rather pessimistic about the upcoming **Unbinding Your Heart** study for the whole church. Today she called me and told me she had been totally wrong. She said she had been in a rut and she is so glad she is participating! Wow!"

We don't need to live our lives as if we're featherweight passengers clinging on to Cherokee's back as he pounds toward the finish line. (I have to say that as I get older, the cosmic "barn" is getting more real and Cherokee doesn't seem to be slowing down!)

Being a Christian offers us more choices than that. We can ask for less passenger mode and more exciting life in Christ. Listen to these powerful things Jesus said:

"… you will know the truth, and the truth will make you free." (John 8:32)

"… the one who believes in me [Jesus] will also do the works that I do and, in fact, will do greater works than these…" (John 14:12)

God can turn us from passengers into riders. Jesus promises that if we follow him, we will live our lives with a profound freedom. Life with Jesus cuts through, "unbinds," the typical constrictions that tie us up and block the effectiveness and joy of our lives. He also says his followers (we, if we choose!) will go greater things than John the Baptist or even Jesus himself! (John 14:12) What do you think about that? Do you believe it?

Listen to St. Paul, one of Jesus' followers, writing about how *his* life feels, "… this one thing I do: forgetting what lies behind and straining forward to what lies ahead, I press on toward the goal for the prize of the heavenly call of God in Christ Jesus." (Phil. 3:13–14)

The apostle Paul isn't ambling through his life, tied up with worries, overwhelmed by events, even when people throw him in prison. He isn't just along for the ride. He isn't watching the race from the sidelines. He doesn't sound like me as the 6th grade passenger. He sounds like Cherokee—heading for the barn, galloping toward God, jumping the fences God's pointing him toward on his way home.

Here's the secret. This religious stuff many of us have heard for years is actually *true*. God exists. We're seeing miraculous movements of the Spirit over and over as we work with hundreds of churches and thousands of individuals. Jesus is alive. God changes lives. We're watching the results of people realizing that their sins are forgiven, that they can live as if they've lost 50 extra pounds—freer, happier, less worried. These truths can set us free to think, to have conversations, to serve other people in ways that matter to God.

God can use us, individually and together in churches, to do miraculous things. God can change our lives, our churches, and the lives of people we don't even *know* yet if we'll pray, ask to be used, and talk with each other for real.

"My mom left me at a church when I was three. She used to travel with the carnival, and the carnival ended up going broke in Iowa. When my mom and my stepfather had a hard day, they'd take it out on me. So she left me at this church with our dog Freddy. She pinned a note on my shirt that said, 'Please take care of her. We can't any longer.'"[2]

— *Brianne Leckness, The Oxford Project*

What's a Relationship with God? What's Prayer?

We shift from passengers to riders as our relationships with God mature. God can begin to help us change when we get brave enough to begin to pray alone, to pray with each other, and to talk about what's really going on in our lives. Changes start when we begin to wonder together—what could *this* mean? What in the world is *this* bit of the Bible saying? Should I take it literally? What's the deep meaning? How could *that* apply to my life? How do I handle *this* challenge? God, what do you want me to do next?

The Bible presents us with all sorts of ways of seeing God, of learning about God. God can communicate with us through the Bible, sometimes in the oddest ways. Prayer gives that process traction.

"I'm so excited about the study and what it's doing in our church. People are increasing in their faith and new things are happening. For example, a layperson preached when our pastor was on vacation last Sunday. Things came out of his mouth about his faith that I NEVER thought I'd hear. I was so excited! I thought, It CAN happen! It CAN happen!"

People pray very differently. Some people sit silently with Scripture and wait for God to illuminate them. Other people share their fears with God as they drive the car. Some ask for help. Others pray out loud in worship. Some people pray aloud in long, poetic paragraphs. A Presbyterian youth group in a downtown church put a bucket of colored chalk on the sidewalk in front of the church, with a sign for the neighbors, "Write your prayers here. We'll pray for each other." The neighbors wrote prayers like, "I lost my job. Please pray for us." "Save my life."

I've heard of people who ask God tiny things, like whether they should paint the living room beige or ecru. Others seem to have a terror of even thinking of approaching God with anything personal. They think it's rude or inappropriate because they perceive God as huge, majestic, distant Father-Creator off in the heavens. Some people adore God. Some praise God. Some leave God severely alone, afraid of being disappointed. Most people would like to know more, but are a little fuzzy on the whole issue.

Who *is* God? God is infinite, immense, powerful—so different from us, so holy, we could be terrified to even say his name out loud. There's a beautiful hymn with the first line, "Immortal, invisible, God only wise."[3] That's the infinite, cosmic, "transcendent" God.

God *also* cares about the tiniest, most personal, silly, details of our lives—if it matters to us, God cares. That's the "pray for your daily bread" God, the God to whom people sing the words "His eye is on the sparrow, I know he watches me."[4] The Bible describes God in both of these ways, and many more—as a wind, as a whisper of a voice, as a mother hen, as a powerful father, as deeper than oceans and creator of the heavens.

The infinite God, Creator of the Universe, came to us as a baby, as a specific person—Jesus. He talked with his friends. He hung out with people he loved. He ate and taught and prayed. Jesus, who is God, had every human emotion we have. He was completely real.

The Holy Spirit comes to us from both God and from Jesus (sometimes Scripture calls the Spirit the "Spirit of God," sometimes, the "Spirit of Christ"). The Holy Spirit lives with us, in us, among us as groups of Christians, more closely than we can image.

God is bigger than we can perceive, creator of infinity, beyond time, creator of life itself. Christ comes to us in time, in a human life like ours. The Spirit offers to lead us, to protect us, encompassed in each moment of our lives, infinitely small and intimate, offering to heal and change and transport us into eternity with God.

If we ask God to show us the next step we need to learn, God will. Do I need to see that God is more majestic, bigger, more "transcendent," than I've ever imagined? God will probably take me there next. If I pray. If I say "yes." Do I need to see that God cares about the tiniest details of my life, that God is "immanent," right here, now? God will probably show me that next. If I pray. If I say "yes."

Whatever we understand about God and ourselves and our lives, it's too small!

But if we will pray, patiently, humbly, daily, reading a bit of the Bible each day, asking God to show us more, to use us, God promises to take us up on it! We don't have to be passive, or helpless, or ineffectual. God can imbue our lives with power and significance, for God's own sake, for God's own purposes.

What would God love to do with you? What could you accomplish, with God, during the rest of your life? What could you learn? What could you do for other people? Visit them in the hospital? Teach someone to read? Play basketball with kids? Go on a retreat and pray for a weekend? Lobby at the state legislature? Participate in a mission trip? Pray for peace? **Work** for peace? Listen to someone? **Really** listen? What kindnesses? What teaching? What sympathy? You possess staggering potential. Your circle of influence is unique. You're the only person who knows your exact collection of friends and coworkers. Most of us are sitting on gifts and potential we don't even **know** about, let alone **use**.

We have a choice. We can ask God to get us in sync with God and with the deepest potential we embody. We can ride peaceably, not fighting the horse, not giving in. We can join up with other riders.

"A couple of groups are now thinking about people outside our church's walls. One Sunday School teacher and his wife (an elder), used the 'interview exercise' from **Unbinding the Gospel** to visit with the Hispanic wait-staff at a local restaurant. The waiters asked them if they would pray for their wives and children they left back in Central America. Our members were very moved by this. They've stayed in contact. They took two Spanish New Testaments to two of the gentlemen last Sunday."

Doesn't that sound better than hanging on for dear life as our lives bolt toward the finish line? The Spirit will guide horses and riders through the right fields, down the right paths, though amazing detours, over huge fences, down sun-dappled lanes, through green pastures at exactly the right pace. God will guide us home to the barn with just the right timing.

Does that sound better than being run away with?

How Do I Get Started?

Testimony in Worship during the E-vent:

"I came to this church a couple of times. Then one of you asked me, 'Why don't you sing in the choir? We'd love to have you.' I said okay, and the choir – and the church – became incredibly important to me. Lots of things came together at the same time, and I started taking care of myself. Over the last couple of years, I've lost 220 pounds. I've been transformed. I'm literally a new person. This is what is possible."

We have discovered that two things help people and churches move closer to Christ. Two action steps can help us shift from drifting to living much more fully into God's power and joy:

1. Talk with each other for real

2. Pray

You can pray with the 40-day prayer journal in this book. If you agree to work through the prayer journal, start tomorrow. Come back and meet again with your group in a week. You'll have prayer experiences and ideas to talk about with each other.

---

[1]Aaron Sorkin, *The West Wing*, Warner Brothers VideoHome, 1999–2006.
[2]Stephen G. Bloom and Peter Feldstein, *The Oxford Project* (New York: Welcome Books, 2008). Quotes from Oxford Project story, CNN.com, October 28, 2008.
[3]"Immortal, Invisible, God Only Wise," words by Walter Chalmers Smith, 1867, Welsh folk melody (St. Denio).
[4]"His Eye Is on the Sparrow," words by Civilla D. Martin, 1905, music by Charles H. Gabriel, 1905, copyright, Hope Publishing Co., 1989.

GROUP DISCUSSION_____

(Light the group's candle to remind all of you that Christ is with you throughout your time. Do this each week.)

1. Open your session with prayer.

2. Introduce yourselves. Go around the group. What are your hopes or expectations for this time together?

3. Look at the covenant at the end of this chapter (page 67). Discuss it. If you feel comfortable, sign it.

Take a Quiz:

Check the statements that describe your life right now:

❏ I'm on an adventure with God.

❏ The horse just bucked me off.

❏ Life's running away with me, and the reins don't work!

❏ I'm watching the horse race on TV.

❏ God, will you give me riding lessons?

Go around the circle and say which answer to this quiz fits you best. Talk about 10 minutes about the chapter and the quiz after everyone has spoken!

Your Group's Foundations:

- Speak honestly.
- Speak and listen in love.
- Explore new ideas.
- Maintain confidentiality.

GROUP EXERCISE _____

(Spend at least half your time on the exercise.)

Divide into triads (groups of three people). Try to be with the people you know least well! Sit comfortably, upright, in silence for two minutes. Ask God to show you a story of God in your life that God would like you to tell these two other people. This could be a profound moment you've remembered forever—a conversion, a healing, some miraculous moment when God felt very near. The Spirit might nudge you to tell some tiny incident you haven't thought of since 4th grade. Don't presume what the story will be—ask God. (God may want you to say some story out loud for your sake. God may wish you to tell it for one of the other two people. Let the Spirit do the choreography.)

Each of you has four minutes to tell your story.

As the other people talk, don't say anything. Don't ask questions. Don't interrupt. Pray for the person speaking. Pray that God will give him/her exactly the right words, and that they will feel Christ's love for them as they trust you enough to say something this important.

Leaders—keep accurate time and signal the end of each time period. Please let people know after three minutes, that they have one more minute to finish their story. Honor the time or we extroverts will trample you introverts! Oops!

Talk as a group about what you learned—about each other, about faith, about God. Did God surprise you by prompting you to tell a story you wouldn't have thought to tell? Were your stories similar? Was another person's story exactly what you needed to hear? What was it like to pray as the other members of your triad talked?

Choose Prayer Partners—exchange phone numbers, arrange for a time to meet during the week (suggestions for your time together are on Day 5 of each week).

Leaders—*pass out white pillar candles that everyone can use during their daily prayer time. Light the candles and pray for each other, for the group, and for how God can use you. If you wish, you could use Prayer Triads (see page 41), then close with prayer for the whole group.*

We can never live in lockstep forever with another person. The only one with whom we can spend our whole life, every minute, inseparably, is God. Each of us can choose to offer our soul and our lives to God, day after day. Prayer is the one-by-one way we communicate with God. God breathes infinity into us through prayer.

GROUP COVENANT

1. Confidentiality. I agree to hold everything said in this group in confidence. I will not repeat anything personal another group member says in the group, or during a private conversation outside the group. I can, of course, talk with people outside the group about how my experience of the group is affecting me, but I will talk about it in a way that won't reveal another group member's confidence.

2. Participation. I'll participate in the four group meetings and have a conversation or meet with my prayer partner three times, between group meetings.

3. Preparation. I'll read the chapter before we meet and do the prayer exercises each day. If a prayer exercise one day makes me crazy, I'll think about why it bothers me, write down why, and pray some other way!

Signature:_____

Date:_____

Steadfast Love, from Everlasting to Everlasting

Scripture: Ephesians 1:15–23

Light your candle to remind yourself that God is with you in your room. Take some slow, deep breaths and relax. Ask God to bless the weeks ahead and your group's study of ***Unbinding Your Soul***.

Let's start with the apostle Paul's great letter to the Ephesians (the church in the Greek city of Ephesus). Paul is Christianity's first great missionary. He left the home he knew, and carried the news of Jesus' ministry, death and resurrection (the "Gospel," the "Good News") beyond Jewish boundaries. He told people from all different backgrounds and countries that the God the Jews worshipped (of whom they may not have heard before) loved them, and offered forgiveness, eternal life and new life to everyone in the world.

This is one of Paul's greatest letters. He doesn't just talk to the Ephesians. His words ring across 2000 years like church bells tolling for us. Scripture is mysterious. Somehow, even though it was written by one man to a specific group of people, it's also written straight from God to us. Will you read Paul's words slowly? Which lines speak to you most powerfully? Mark them. Sit quietly for a moment. Now read it again, slowly. What words or phrases shine out at you ***this*** time? Mark them or write them down.

What in this passage do you **_know_** to be true? Write down Paul's words that you've experienced yourself in half the space below.

Now read Paul's words again and underline the phrases you'd ***like*** to know to be true, or to experience yourself, or to understand better. Write those on the other side of your writing space. Make a small mark next to the one or two huge truths that you most want to know in your own life.

Will you ask God to show you?

Notes, lists, drawings, ideas:

Prayer: God, you are the Holy One of Israel. I praise and bless you. Thank you for showing me the beginnings of the boundless love you have for all people, even for me. Will you give me some specific pictures or ideas of what these words and phrases _____ _____ could mean in my life? Will you help me to know these huge truths better over the next weeks? Thank you. Amen.

Look Back at Yesterday. Now, Go On!

Scripture: Micah 7:18–20

We're all partial, fragile and don't meet even our ***own*** expectations. How must God see us! Yet over and over, God loves us. God sees us exactly as we are and loves us more than we can imagine. Read these words from the prophet Micah. Prophets see situations very clearly. They continually tell us how God sees us. Prophets aren't always so comfortable to be around, but they help us grow. A friend used to say that it's only your best friends who will tell you that you have spinach between your teeth. Prophets tell you about the spinach! Read the words of Micah, one of the Old Testament prophets. Do you see God's clear-sightedness? Do you get ideas about God's mercy?

Sit quietly for a few moments. Breathe and relax. Feel what is true—God is all around you. Read the Micah text again. Ask God to walk through the last 24 hours with you, hour by hour. Ask God to help you remember each moment of grace, forgiveness, blessing, learning, of God's presence, or other people's love. Write them down in a list. Thank God for them.

Ask God to show you the moments in the day when you were farthest from God, the moment you'd most like to do differently. Ask God's forgiveness. Give thanks and ask to go into this next day forgiven, restored and happy!

Notes, drawings, insights, thoughts:

Prayer: Beloved God, thank you for these times today when I have felt close to you, or sensed your action: _____.
Please forgive me for these times when I've fallen short: _____
_____. Help me to do better tomorrow. Bless those I've been with today. Bless and prepare my way into the situations and people I'll meet tomorrow. Amen.

The Jesus Prayer

Scripture: 1 Thessalonians 5:16–22

Supplies: *a string of pearls or beads—Mardi Gras beads, Eastern Orthodox prayer beads—anything to hold in your hands, to pass from one hand to another. Or be ready to walk. Or to sit and breathe!*

What did Paul mean when he said to "pray without ceasing"? Many Eastern Orthodox monks believe that if we pray simply and often enough, we begin to pray all the time. Our hearts beat in time with the prayer, our breath is synchronized with it. They pray the "Jesus Prayer."

The prayer is very simple: *Lord Jesus Christ, Son of God, have mercy on me, a sinner.*

Some people pray the prayer without the last phrase, "a sinner." You choose, or experiment with both. You can pray this prayer many, many ways. I love to pray holding a string of some kind of beads. Hold the first bead and think "Lord Jesus Christ" and inhale very slowly. As you exhale slowly, think "Son of God." Inhale with "have mercy on me," and exhale with "a sinner." Shift that bead into your right hand (or left, if you are left-handed) and pray the same way on the second bead.

You can pray without the beads, just using your breath to feel the rhythm of the prayer. You can whisper the words. You can walk and take a step for each of the four "steps" of the prayer. Pray the Jesus Prayer for a long time. When you are finished, thank God.

Notes, drawings, thoughts:

Prayer: Lord Jesus Christ
              Son of God
              Have mercy on me
              A sinner.

The Jesus Prayer, Russian Orthodox Church

Char's Prayers

Scripture: Colossians 1:9–14; 4:2–4

My friend Don was a gifted and a little-bit-wild California kid who lived in a tough family situation. When he was nine years old, his best friend's mom was prompted to pray for Don every day. She told him about it when he was in his teens. Don is now 67. Char is 90. In those 58 years, Char has prayed for Don every day. In those years, Don became a surfer and skier. His plane circled the Bay of Pigs, as Don and his paratrooper friends waited for the plane to drop them into Cuba. In the army, he accepted Christ, then went to college, and later became a pastor. His three adult sons are amazing people. He is one of the most powerful, and authentic, Christians I have ever known. Don's life has influenced tens of thousands of people. I'm one of them. Char's prayers, day, after day, after tens of thousands of days, have undergirded it all.

We are called to pray for each other. Read Paul's words to the Colossians. We must pray for each other—for knowledge of God's will, that we may lead lives worthy of the Lord, that we may bear fruit, that we may be strong, patient and enduring. We must pray for openings to speak of the mystery of Christ. Prayer matters more than we will ever know.

Will you ask God for whom you can pray? Don't presume you know whom God will want you to pray for—ask! You may know the person. You may not. It could be your next-door neighbor. It could be all of the 11th graders in the high school you drive past every day on the way to work. Just ask God, "Who?" Write down the name or a description here. Will you pray for this person each day for the next week?

Notes, lists, drawings, ideas:

Prayer: Oh Holy One of Israel, I praise you! Thank you for the people who have prayed for me during my life. Will you show me for whom you want *me* to pray? *(Wait with God in silence.)* I hold this person as if it were your arms around them, Lord. Bless them. Keep them safe. Give them moments today of being more and more aware of you. Thank you, God. Amen.

A Prayer Partner Day

Scripture: Luke 10:1–12

Jesus asks the disciples to do ministry in pairs. Paul did ministry with others—with Barnabas (a peer), with Timothy (a young man), with Prisca and Aquilla (a married couple). We can't live Christian lives alone. No matter how much we pray, no matter how much we love God, being a Christian means we get to live with other people. We learn from them. We do work together. They learn to love us enough to be honest with us and to hold us accountable. We can help them. We are Christ's hands and eyes and feet in this world, but like a hand, an eye, or a foot, we live as half of a pair. You may annoy your partner to distraction, but by the grace of God, s/he will learn a lot just by being in relationship with you! *And*, you'll do better work together than separately.

Look at this passage in Luke—Jesus sent out 70 followers in pairs to preach that the Kingdom of God was near. They were to heal and preach and pray with people. It would be dangerous—they were "like lambs in the midst of wolves." Doing what Jesus asks of us can be a scary adventure. It's best to do it together.

Meet with your prayer partner today. (You can always switch prayer partner days to fit your schedules.) Talk about how your prayers have gone this week. What has happened? What are you learning? What's really pushing you in this process? What feels like you were born to do it? Whom are you feeling called to pray for together? (The group? The church? A situation you're aware of? Specific people? Children in your town?) Ask how you can pray for your prayer partner during the coming week. Let your partner know how s/he can pray for you.

Pray together for the situations you've identified.

Notes, lists, drawings, ideas:

I am praying for _____
this week.

Reflection Day

Read. Have you read chapter 6 so you're ready for tomorrow's group meeting?

Review. Think back over your week of prayer. Reread your favorite scripture from the week. Review your notes, lists, insights. How is your prayer life going? Review *Using Your Prayer Journal,* beginning on page 123. Which ideas do you need to pay particular attention to this week? Take some notes.

Pray for the person you discerned you should pray for on Day 4.

Then, answer two questions:

Question 1: *What are the most important things you've learned/discovered/remembered this week?*

Question 2: *What do you wonder about?*

I am praying for _____this week.

Prayer: Talk to God. Sit in silence for a bit. Listen. Amen.

Reframe…

*Dave is a retired advertising executive, a pillar of his congregation. He told his pastor that he had to quit the group study of **Unbinding the Gospel** two days after the first group meeting. "I can't do this. Evangelism is why I left the Southern Baptist church 20 years ago. I have taken the training. I've heard the sermons. I don't have the gift of evangelism. I felt so guilty about it I had to shift to a denomination where evangelism isn't an issue. Now we're doing it **here**! I can't do this. I've tried and I can't even stand to sit in this group." The pastor said he understood and told Dave to do what he had to do.*

A couple of days later, Dave took one of his friends with him to serve meals to hungry people. The church feeds about 350 people a week. Dave told his friend on the drive over, "This is the greatest deal. I love serving these meals. I do it every week, and it's one the most meaningful things I do. It's just great! You're going to like this." They went. They served lunches. They had a wonderful afternoon. Dave dropped his friend off and headed home himself.

Then it hit him. He'd just done evangelism. It's faith sharing. It's life sharing. Hmmmmm… Reframe. Reframe.

He rejoined his study group.

CHAPTER 6

The Great Toxic Word

(If you weren't raised in church, you might as well just read this chapter for its informational and entertainment value.)

I've led research projects and done practical revitalization work with thousands of normal Christians and pastors, seminary professors and bishops for 15 years.[1] Here's one key finding of years of evangelism research: You cannot overestimate the toxicity of the word "evangelism." No matter how cautiously you say it, the Great Toxic Word drives church people up the wall. The Word is the verbal equivalent of an invitation to a picnic on the dirt at Chernobyl.

Say the Word—people may look calm, but their ears tell their brains that you've transmuted into Freddy Krueger. Keep talking after you let the Hideous Word loose and people might as well have their hands over their ears, muttering, "LALALALALALALALALA……"

Once it's spoken, no one can hear anything that's said next. Here it is. Whisper it out loud to yourself and see if you flinch:

I have seen one thing over and over as I've worked with people and churches. If we honestly ask God to come into our hearts, God will. If we honestly ask God to help us love other people and be sensitive to what they really need, God will. If we ask God to use us to help other people, inside and beyond church walls, to discover the power of a life of faith, God will.

evangelism

See?

Alright. We need to get past this. What do you think when you hear the word "evangelism?" No, what do you *really* think? Write it down on the next page.

Good to get that out of your system? Feel like a whole new person?

Excellent.

"The first day of our all-church study of **Unbinding Your Heart,** a group leader heard four of our members climbing the stairs to class, muttering, 'I didn't read it; did you?' 'I'm not doing evangelism. I can't stand this touchy-feely stuff.' 'The last thing I need today is a séance.'

On the way out of the group meeting: 'I had no idea Bill had been through that.' 'This was amazing.' 'All right. I'll do it.'"

What did you write? Our research showed that a dreaded collection of cartoon images of evangelism haunts the minds of most people who grew up in churches. It's probably a version of post-traumatic stress disorder. Whisper "evangelism" into the ear of someone who grew up in a church and

- Adrenaline rushes into their systems (it tastes bitter)
- They break out in a cold sweat
- Stomachs churn as their minds are swamped with horrifying pictures of
  ~ Sitting in a locked room, memorizing a training flip chart that will manipulate you to argue friends into positions
  ~ A blonde, buxom TV evangelist crying and batting inch-long eyelashes
  ~ Peer pressure forcing you to stuff tracts into strangers' tremulous hands
  ~ Knocking on neighbors' doors on a Saturday morning to beat them about the head and shoulders with biblical proof-texts
  ~ Making your friends uncomfortable
  ~ People mocking you behind your back

Take a breath. We need to get past this.

Let's talk about what we discovered in the huge, four-year study of evangelism in churches all over the country.[2] We studied churches that are doing exciting, vibrant, statistically effective faith sharing. We discovered that evangelism ("faith sharing," if you prefer) that actually **works** has nothing to do with the bad cartoons lurking in the corners of Christians' minds. Here's what statistically effective faith sharing (evangelism) **does** look like:

- People who love God listen to other people prayerfully and are real friends, available for significant conversations.

- If the Spirit prompts them, they say something about what God has done in their lives, or offer to pray for their friend, or ask the person if they'd like to connect with some group in their church.

Do you remember the exercises you all did last week, when you told each other a story of God in your lives? …when you listened and prayed for the other person as they talked? That's what we're talking about. That is the heart of evangelism. You already did it, so everybody can calm down!

All we need to do is be aware of God in our lives. We can pray. We can talk with each other about our faith inside church so that your church is actually a vibrant spiritual community. Who wouldn't want to be part of *that*?

What Is Evangelism?

For this book, evangelism is anything you do to help another person move closer to a relationship with God, or into Christian community.

We can let God change us, day by day into the loving, powerful, faith-filled people God dreams of us each being. God wants us to love others, to care that our lives and theirs are as full of meaning as they can be. Full lives, meaningful lives, involve a relationship with God. God offers that relationship to us. We get to talk with our friends about it.

I have seen one thing over and over as I've worked with people and churches. If we honestly ask God to come into our hearts, God will. If we honestly ask God to help us love other people and be sensitive to what they really need, God will. If we ask God to use us to help other people, inside and beyond church walls, to discover the power of a life of faith, God will.

God will fulfill our most tentative requests in ways we could never imagine or anticipate. God will perform miracles through us, not because we're so cool, but because God is the God of infinite love and possibilities, because God is the God of overwhelming power and mystery.

If we are the slightest bit willing, if we crack open the door of our souls to God, we have no idea what could happen. All we have to do is to begin to want to ask.

A Disciples of Christ church decided to buy an old Wal-Mart building to start a new congregation. They aimed it, with blaring music, at 20-somethings. They ended up with huge numbers of empty nesters, Baby Boomers. (I suspect that these 50 and 60-year-olds were raised on a diet of high-decibel Stones' concerts, so requests to turn up the music from this congregation may be both a function of musical taste and hearing loss. I'm just wondering here.)

One of the pastors said that a lot of these people "are looking at their lives with regret about not having raised their kids in the church. The kids' lives are out of control—under 30, on second divorce and with $80,000 in credit card debt. We're seeing that the longer people have been away from church, the harder it is for them to take the scary step to come back. We love these people. We can't wait to connect with them, and their kids."

Did you watch the track and field events in the 2008 Beijing Olympics? For the first time since 1928, no U.S. team competed in the finals of the 400 relay. The most gifted track and field runners in the world—individually—filled the spots on the U.S. team. But they weren't coordinated. They changed coaches mid-stream. They changed who was going to run which race. They didn't practice the handoffs. They dropped the baton in the semifinals! And they blew it, big time.

"We hosted a 'Name Your Tattoo' party. You have no idea how significant people's tattoos are to them! From the WWII sailor to the 16-year-old whose mother wasn't all that thrilled with the new dolphin on Becky's arm, we heard stories about crucial times in people's lives. (We did establish some anatomical parameters about where the tattoos could be!)"

Those of you who base your lives on God, on the faith, think hard. What do God and your faith mean to you? Why does it matter that you are a Christian? Why would it matter to anyone else? This is a movement, a movement of the Spirit. If we truly are basing our lives on our faith, mightn't that living relationship with God be important to someone else we know?

We have the rest of our lives, individually and collectively, to think about it, to do something about it, to practice the handoffs.

Amy signed up for an *Unbinding* group in her United Church of Christ church because she thought it was about prayer. (It is.) She opened her copy of **Unbinding Your Heart**, saw the great toxic word, "evangelism," and wanted to run for the hills. "I want no part of this. I didn't sign up for evangelism." Then she thought, "Well, I'll just do the prayer journal in the back." She started praying and liked it. Her daughter was being bullied at school. The family was very concerned about it, had taken action to get it stopped, but nothing helped.

As she read the exercise on the fourth day of the prayer journal ("Prayer for the Children"), Amy decided to pray about the bullying. She prayed that God would help stop the bullying. She prayed for protection for her daughter. The next day, *the Very Next Day*, the ringleader of the bullying called her daughter and apologized.

Amy went to work the next day and told everyone in her office about it—the bullying, the prayer, and the next day, out-of-the-blue apology. Their jaws dropped. One of the other women in the office told everyone that **her** daughter was being bullied too. She asked Amy to pray for **her** child. Amy said, "Well, sure. This is amazing. Prayer actually works! Of **course**, I'll pray for your daughter."

On the way home she thought, "Oh my **gosh**! That was **evangelism**! Duhh—faith sharing is just talking about what's true! I not only **could** do that, **I DID** it!"

Do you know what else we discovered during four years of research into superb evangelism, effective faith sharing? The people who get upset by the idea of evangelism are the ones who grew up in churches. Even teens and 20-somethings raised in the church share the 60-year-olds' discomfort. New Christians and Christians who keep discovering deeper layers of spiritual reality don't have much trouble listening to their friends talk about substantial issues, or telling their friends what they experience in their faith lives.

Isn't that interesting?

You can tell congregations to "go be missional" until the cows come home. If they aren't internally motivated to share their faith, they just won't do it. Once we know **why** to share our faith, we'll figure out **how** in organic ways that work.

---

[1]The Mainline Evangelism Project was a major, four-year study of highly effective evangelism in seven mainline denominations, made possible by a grant from the Lilly Endowment, Martha Grace Reese, Project Director. Congregations studied were affiliated with the American Baptist Churches, USA, Christian Church (Disciples of Christ), Evangelical Lutheran Church in America, Presbyterian Church USA, Reformed Church in America, United Church of Christ and The United Methodist Church. See *Unbinding the Gospel*, 2nd ed. (St. Louis: Chalice Press, 2008) and go to *www.GraceNet. info* for general information on the purpose of the study. The Wenger-Reese sociological report (more detailed statistical results of the Mainline Evangelism Project) is available at *www.GraceNet.info / Download Resources*.

[2]See previous note.

Giggling, dodging and weaving through Barnes & Noble

A pastor put the following note in the church newsletter:

"Buy a Starbucks gift card. Leave it in a book at Barnes & Noble. Attach this note, in your writing, 'Enjoy a beverage on me. Look over one of these books while you do so. Bless you, _____—A friend from Westminster Presbyterian on _____ Road.'"

A member in the church sent this e-mail to the pastor that week:

"Just wanted to share this with you. Lucy and I had lunch today at Starbucks in Barnes & Noble. We purchased the $5.50 gift cards and left them with a note hidden amongst the books. We had such fun doing that—it filled my heart with joy. We were giggling like teenagers when we left! Also, we ran into a couple of other people from our church who were either on the same mission or checking on gift cards they had left a few days ago.

Before I left to meet my adventurous cohort, I was talking to my sister in Jacksonville and told her I had to "run an errand for Jesus." So of course, I had to explain what I was doing. She liked the idea of the gift cards so much she is going to tell her preacher and Sunday School teacher about it. She thinks they will probably do something like that too…Anyway, just wanted to share our experience with you. Hope we can do some more fun things for Jesus."

GROUP DISCUSSION_____

1. Start with Prayer Triads (page 41).

2. What has God done during your prayer times this week?

3. What do you think about evangelism? Really! What did you write on page 76 in response to the word, "evangelism?" Do you notice a difference between people in your group who were raised in the church (or had strong church experiences in the past) and those who are fairly new to churches and faith?

4. Would you feel comfortable with a humbler idea of faith sharing? How about asking friends who don't go to church to help you see the world, God, faith and church with their eyes? Your group could invite friends who are interested in spirituality but who don't go to a church to join this group. Then you could all pray together and talk about faith issues on an equal footing, with deep respect. See what the Spirit can do in each of your lives. How threatening is that idea? Does it sound like fun? What scares you about it? What excites you about it?

GROUP EXERCISE _____

Divide into groups of three or four. Try to make the numbers between groups even. Sit quietly for a couple of minutes. Ask God to help you get a real answer to whichever question fits you better:

Q. 1 "What difference does it make in your life that you are a Christian? Why does it matter?"

<u>*or*</u>

Q. 2 "How might my life be different if I *were* a Christian?"

Take a couple of minutes each to talk about it. Then combine into the full group and talk more.

Now sit in silence and ask God to show you some people you know who might be interested in trying an experiment in Christian prayer and community—three weeks of prayer and four weeks of being part of a group like this one.

Pray together for the people who occurred to you during the silence. Pray for each other and for what God can do with each of your lives.

> "A woman I consider a saint shared her story. We were all in tears. We had gone to countless church dinners, programs, meetings and services. We had never done something as simple as sharing what Christ means in our lives. Just doing that was more powerful than I ever could have imagined."
>
> —*Male elder, Reformed Church in America*

A Literal Baton Pass—Bless the Books

Take a fresh copy of *Unbinding Your Soul* that a new person *could* use if your group decides to keep going and invite friends to do Part One, The Experiment, with you. You probably don't know who should have the book yet. You may not even be the person who issues the invitation. But each of you, sit, holding a book for a new person. Close your eyes and pray that the book will get to the right person.

Keep praying for the person each day during your prayer times for the next two weeks. Hold the book and pray that *if* it's right for them to be part of this group, they'll say "yes." Pray that God will make the time exactly what they need it to be if they agree to do The Experiment. Pray that your group will be sensitive, powerful, thoughtful, open, creative and fun.

If someone else occurs to you during your prayer, pray for both people. Let the Spirit prompt your prayer. God may want you to invite two people to join you.

Discuss: Discuss, without deciding, whether you might want to continue this group at the end of your four weeks. You could each ask someone new into a four-session, three-weeks-of-prayer opportunity, using chapters 1-4 of *Unbinding Your Soul*. What do you think? Don't decide, just mull it over together.

> "These books are not really about evangelism as much as they're about unfreezing icy hearts. The real focus is to invite people to try God again for the first time. When our hearts begin to thaw through the practice of the spiritual exercises, we're open to God and others in ways we never imagined possible. The serendipitous result is the inclusion of new people into the faith."
>
> *—United Methodist pastor*

ASSIGNMENT FOR THE WEEK _____

Pray each day this week for the people who came to mind as you prayed just now. Ask God if you should think about inviting them to join this group in a week or so.

Joy in Your Life

Scripture: Habakkuk 3:17–19; Galatians 5:22–25

Light your candle. Ask Christ to be very near and to help you see what he'd like you to see during this prayer time. Now read this scripture from the Jewish prophet Habakkuk. He's not just describing his life and emotions. All of chapter 3 is a prayer. Habakkuk says that even during disaster he will rejoice in and exult in the God of his salvation. Habakkuk says (and prays) that God is his strength and that God makes him leap like a deer and jump to the heights. What??? Can you believe anyone can feel joy in the midst of destruction? Read his words again. What do you think?

Can you remember a great joy in your life—not just surface happiness, but a deep, wellspring of joy? Have you ever experienced a joy so profound it felt like a force of nature, not just an emotion? Or a joy so subtle you can't explain or express it? Have you ever fallen in love? Won the play-off game? Had a child? Have you ever experienced joy that comes even more directly from your relationship with God? Watched a friend be baptized? … asked God for forgiveness and realized you really were forgiven and could start fresh? … felt a sense of Christ with you? …connected with someone as you talk about faith? Sang a song that overwhelmed you with God's love?

What if you let God even *more* into your life, so that this deep joy could come more and more often from God? Deep joy is a fruit of the Spirit (Galatians 5:22-25). That means the Holy Spirit will "grow" joy in us as we mature as Christians. Joy is actually a "by-product" of a spiritual faith. Do you want to ask God for a deeper, more direct relationship that will make real joy possible?

Sit quietly. Read the scripture again. Ask Christ/God/the Spirit if you should ask for this deeper relationship. When you're ready, ask God to come closer. Say, "Yes."

Notes, lists, drawings, ideas:

Insight: "Joy is prayer—Joy is strength—Joy is love—Joy is a net of love by which you can catch souls." *Mother Teresa of Calcutta, Albanian-born Roman Catholic missionary (1910-1997)*

Prayer: God, please send your Holy Spirit into my life. I ask to know you better. Help me rely on you more. I ask for your Spirit and the gift of your joy. Amen.

Connect the Dots!

Scripture: Genesis 5:21–24

Do you ever feel as if your life's made up of little compartments? There's the work you, the Little League coach you, the family you, the church you, the hang-around-with-friends you? You're the same person, but every place you go sees a little different side of you. My mother-in-law was the principal of a preschool program for over 30 years. Her four- and five-year-old students used to skid to a halt when they saw her in the grocery store on a Saturday. "Wait! Mrs. White's in the Wrong Place! She lives at school!"

Okay, how much of your spiritual life "lives at church?" How completely does your faith connect with your family life? Estimate the percentages of your "faith self" that you take into other areas of your life: To work? %_____ To a ballgame? %_____ Out for a drink with friends? %_____. Estimate the percentage of your "faith self" that functions Monday-Saturday: %_____.

The goal of Christian maturity is to be pretty much the same person as you travel between the worlds in which you live. Look at the way the writer of Genesis described Methuselah's father, Enoch: "Enoch walked with God." What would it be like to be aware of walking with God every step of your life? (Genesis says "*walked* with God," not "talked *about* God." Don't race off and do something rash. This is a *prayer* connection.)

Will you try something today? ***Pray that today you will walk with God.*** Here are some suggestions: Pray in your office. Pray for the people in the restaurant around you. Pray for the other kids in your class, or for all the employees at the grocery store. Pray for your children as you watch TV this evening. You could pray for each person whose mailing label you put on an envelope. Someone might start a conversation about a real life, faith issue. If so, you might say what you think out of your experience. But the goal here is for you to be aware of walking with God. You don't need to say a word. Just connect dots in your own head.

What happened? Notes, drawings, thoughts:

Insight: "In the sermon… I spake [spoke]…from Genesis 5:24, "And Enoch walked with God." I was sweetly assisted [by God] to insist on a close walk with God, and to leave this as my parting advice to God's people here, that they should walk with God."

David Brainerd, American missionary, 1718-1747

Jesus Stops to Listen to Me

Scripture: John 5:1–9

Sit. Ask the Spirit to show you what you need to see or hear in this scripture. Then slowly read John 5:1-9, the story of Jesus healing a paralyzed man. Reread the scripture and write what occurs to you.

Imagine that you are the paralyzed man. Sit in your chair, or lie down. Imagine that you can't move. Feel what it would be like to have been lying helpless for 38 years. Have you almost given up hope of being healed? Everyone keeps rushing past to take their own sick friends into the pool, but you've been lying there, ignored, passed over. Think how that feels.

Then Jesus comes to talk with you. Jesus stops everything. He looks straight at you. He talks directly to you. What does he say? What do *you* want to say to him? Say it. Then Jesus heals you. Jesus will listen to the deepest needs of our souls. Jesus will hear you now. Tell him whatever lies on your heart.

Your words are prayer.

Notes, drawings, thoughts:

Prayer: Thank you, Jesus, for really hearing what I say, even if I can't put it into words. Please heal me. Amen.

Listening "in Christ"

Scripture: *2 Corinthians 3:18; Galatians 2:19–20; 1 John 3:23–24*

Something happens when we go through life as Christians. We change if we allow the Holy Spirit to work with us. Paul says that as we see the glory of the Lord, we "are being transformed into the same image from one degree of glory to another" (2 Corinthians 3:18) and "I have been crucified with Christ; and it is no longer I who live, but it is Christ who lives in me" (Galatians 2:19-20). St. John tells us that all who obey God's commandments "abide in him, and he abides in them" (1 John 3:24). We change and become more like Christ as we mature and walk more closely with God. We never get perfect, but God can work with us. Christ can work through us.

Remember how it felt when you spoke with Jesus yesterday? When he listened?

Jesus loves each of us and listens to us with great love. As Christ and the Spirit begin to transform us, **we** become more Christ-like. Then we can give that gift of listening with love to each other. We can learn to listen with Christ's ears, to see people with Christ's eyes, instead of **looking** as if we're listening, but secretly thinking about what we're going to say next. Do you ever look over someone's shoulders at the sports bar to see what the Yankees are doing? That's probably not what Jesus would do. (My husband says he'd be pullling for the Angels.)

Will you give the gift of Christ-like listening to someone today? During one or two conversations today, even on the phone, ask Christ to help you listen. Pray for the person while they're talking. (Don't close your eyes or anything, but feel as if you are asking God to help them say exactly what they mean. Pray that they will feel Christ's presence, ask the Spirit to give them the right words, and for them to feel God's love, even if they aren't conscious of it. Ask Christ to "listen through you" and to let you hear what they're **really** saying, including the sub-text.)

How was it different from a normal talk?

Notes, drawings, thoughts, insights:

Prayer: Lord, please hear the words and the needs of _____, whom you and I listened to today. Please tell me now anything about them I didn't hear clearly. Let me know how to pray **with you** for them. [Listen to Jesus.] Amen.

Praying in Spiritual Agreement

Scripture: Matthew 18:15–20

Prepare to meet your prayer partner: Sit quietly. Then read the scripture carefully. I have written a bit about my understanding of this passage in **Unbinding the Gospel**. I am reprinting it on the next page, because spiritual agreement is a crucial prayer dynamic. Read page 88 now, please. Now reread Matthew 18:15-20. How does this passage strike you? Think about it—write a bit.

Close your eyes and take several minutes to pray silently. Empty your mind; breathe slowly and deeply. After you feel centered, ask if there is any person or situation God would like you to pray for when you meet with your prayer partner. Write the names down.

Time with your prayer partner: Meet with your prayer partner. Review how your prayer for each other has gone during the last week. How are those situations? Would it help to pray the same prayer, or differently for each other in the coming week?

Discuss today's preparation prayer and the idea of "spiritual agreement." Talk about the situations you discerned you should pray about. Discuss what the real issues are—and **how** to pray. **What's the situation?** …a friend at school who's flirting with risky behavior? **How should you pray for him/her?** It's best to try to figure out the core of what's going on. Might it be better to pray that he'll find a deeper relationship with Christ and be drawn to healthier friends? Would it be good to pray that his parents develop more patience and a greater sense of detachment? Talk about it with your partner. You may have an "a-*ha!*" moment.

When you're in agreement about **how** to pray, pray together for these people/situations. You could sit together and pray silently, or you may pray out loud (or both). Then keep praying about the situation during the coming week.

Notes, drawings, thoughts:

Prayer: I'm praying for:_____

Quote from *Unbinding the Gospel:*
(Read with prayer exercise for Week E, Day 5 Prayer Journal)

In Matthew 18, Jesus tells the disciples, "Whatever you bind on earth will be bound in heaven, and whatever you loose on earth will be loosed in heaven" (Mt. 18:18). *We* are also given the power to untie or unbind things. As disciples of Christ, we have the power to affect great things. Later in the scripture, Jesus says, "If two of you agree on earth about anything you ask, it will be done for you by my Father in heaven" (Matthew 18:19).

*My friend Don Schutt [remember prayer exercise Week D, Day 4?] is certain Jesus could make this promise because it's so hard to get two or three people to agree about **anything**! Don says, more seriously, that this mysterious passage means that if we try to discern the deep realities of a situation so that we can pray about it together, in sync with God's will, that it enables God to use our prayer to accomplish God's desires. If we will think about a situation, pray to understand it, talk together and pray in the agreement of the understanding the Spirit has given us, our prayer will be Christ's prayer....*

Many of the dear churches we love are inflexible. Many churches are tied into knots of self-involvement or old habit. Most of us are fairly knotted up as people. We're anxious, worried, stewing, angry or afraid. The Gospel is about freedom in Christ. Think of all the strands that tie us up—death, sin, fear, anger, addictions, nasty gossiping, fussy tediousness, age-old resentments, self-involvement! The Gospel, the Good News, is about freedom in Christ. It is about knots being untied, ropes loosened, ties unbound.

Every one of us is too narrow in our understanding. We don't want upsets in our lives, or changes in our habits, or threats to our opinions. Shifting from Shredded Wheat™ to oatmeal exhausts me on a bad day! ...Do you dare risk agreeing with some others in your church to pray together and see what God can do? Do you dare not risk it?[1]

---

[1]Martha Grace Reese, *Unbinding the Gospel,* 2nd ed. (St. Louis: Chalice Press, 2008), pp. 54-55. Used with permission, emphasis added.

Review & Thinking Day

Read. Have you read chapter 7 so you're ready for tomorrow's group meeting?

Review. Think back over your week of prayer. Reread your favorite scripture from the week. Review your notes, lists, insights. How is your prayer going? Review *Using Your Prayer Journal,* beginning on page 123. Which ideas do you need to pay particular attention to this week? Take some notes.

Then, answer two questions:

Question 1: What are the most important things you've learned/discovered/remembered this week?

Question 2: What are you thinking about most? What question do you have?

I'm praying for:_____

Prayer: Talk to God. Sit in silence. Listen. Amen.

Say it in words…

Mary, her husband and two children moved to Oak Bluff. Mary's a beautician. Have you ever had your hair cut? You know how hairdressers tend to be not so shy? They ask you about your life. You get to hear about their new puppy and what the kids are doing. It's great to get your hair done. You hear the next installment. You get to talk about your life. You only pay for the shampoo and cut, not for the therapy. Someone who cares is listening!

About a year after Mary and her family moved, her husband left her. Her clients were wonderful. One of them brought her a couple of bags of groceries. Another gave her some of her kids' outgrown clothes. One called out over the blow-dryer, "Why don't you let me take care of the kids when you go to the lawyer's office tomorrow?" Mary talked. People listened. They were wonderful.

The kids were with their dad one weekend. Mary walked around her neighborhood on the verge of tears. She passed a church on the corner and thought, "I ought to try to go to church. I liked it that year I was 12 and went with Brittany's family. Maybe that would help."

She got up at eight the next morning. Squadrons of butterflies did double gainers with a twist in her stomach as she got closer and closer to THE CHURCH. It was huge. It was scary. She stopped at the curb.

A couple of teenagers ran out the front doors and came up to talk with her. "Hey! How are you? Come on in! Have you been here before? Wait! You're Tom's mom, aren't you? We're really glad you're here!!" They swooped her up to a couple of people at the front door. Those people gave her a bulletin, showed her the coat rack, took her in and introduced her to Sue, who was sitting halfway down the aisle on the left.

Sue was great. The service was powerful. Mary heard a terrific sermon and music she liked. There wasn't too much stuff that made her feel as if she didn't know what was going on. (Anyway, Sue was there, explaining.) Mary loved it. Halfway through the service, she spotted the client who had offered to watch her kids during the lawyer's appointment on Thursday. Three minutes later, she saw the woman who had brought her groceries and the family that had given her their kids' outgrown clothes. Five of her clients were in the sanctuary. The sixth one always went to the 11 o'clock service.

How many of them had been wonderful to her? All six.
How many of them had shown beautiful Christian love to her? All six.
How many of them had invited her to church? None.
How many of them had mentioned that they were Christians? None.

CHAPTER 7

Connect the Dots

Sunday........Wednesday
Oasis...........Desert

The members of a huge Lutheran church in the Minneapolis area committed themselves in January 2009. They decided that during the economic downturn, no one in the church is going to go without food, without a roof over their heads, or without someone to walk with them. Families are inviting other families to live with them for a while. Now that's a ***church***. Churches can be awesome!

Does your church welcome you like a traveler arriving at an oasis? Do you get through your week, walk into church and feel safe from the craziness? …among friends? …as if God and these fabulous people are filling you up with fuel to get you through ***next*** week?

Most of us love our churches. I relax when I see people who know me well, love me in spite of how I am. These are the folks I ***know*** I can lean into when times get tough. I think of church, and I conjure up memories of friends turning around, waving and grinning across the sanctuary. I think of quiet times of prayer—alone in the chapel, together with a group of Christians who will lay their lives on the line for Christ. I think of Mae Ringham, 83 years old and weighing in at about 83 pounds. When I was a young pastor/mom, Mae made her angel food cake for church suppers and always saved back a piece for me because I loved it. We all need a mom to protect us.

What do you think of when you think of your church? …being accepted after you drank again? …getting to work with the third

We tame what church can be. We try to tame who Christ is. For many of us, Jesus is an historical figure we "believe in." That's true, but he's also a living, risen vibrant force. If we say yes, he'll be a power in our lives, not some vaguely comforting idea in the backs of our minds.

graders? …the excitement of joining in on a mission trip? …the place where you meet Christ? …the place where you can talk about **anything**?

What's **your** picture of **your** church, your faith community? If you aren't connected with a church, what's your **idea** of church? Do you have an ideal? Have you had a bad experience with a church that soured that ideal? What do you think about the group with which you're studying **Unbinding Your Soul?** Think about what's in your head, your heart and your memory when you think about church. Write your first thoughts here:

"Our *Unbinding* group started praying for friends who don't go to church. We have no logical idea how it happened, but stuff about faith, or church just started coming up in conversations we had with these people in the next weeks. So we invited them. I guess connecting our faith with people outside the church is where the rubber meets the road, isn't it?"

Let's shift gears. Have you ever had the feeling of being a different person in different places? Maybe you **are** a teenager. If you aren't, I'll bet money you **remember**! You know the peer pressure thing? Most of us, kids and adults, adapt to our settings. We adopt a protective coloration, camouflage. We try to blend in.

Ever been the nerdy guy in a group of jocks? What did you do? Become the manager of the baseball team, or learn to be funny?

Have you ever been the good kid surrounded by others who weren't so studious? Get stuffed in your locker for raising your hand in class? Were you the girl who had had sex with a bunch of boyfriends, while the other girls were Sunday School innocents? … chubby among the models? … new kid in the middle of the school year? …from a different **country**? Ouch!

The thought of not fitting in, of not being one of the cool kids **still** can make you squirm! We're built to have friends. We're built to adapt to our settings. We yearn to fit in, to find an oasis of safety, of friends. We **learn** to fit in, to seem not too different, to adopt the protective coloration of the group in which we find ourselves. Good or bad (and it's usually both), we find ways to exist within our contexts. Most of us do a better job of being our "real" selves in different contexts as we mature, but we all adapt to our settings. It's good to adapt to our settings in lots of ways. But we can leave important parts of ourselves in the car when we go into different buildings—home, church, office, the bar.

Most of us act nicer in church, tougher at the office, let down our hair at parties, and who knows what at home! You know what I'm talking about? We compartmentalize our lives. You probably wouldn't swear with a group of your church friends. You probably go into intense, organized work mode at work, or hide your private, "real" self. In our heads, we leave things in their own little places. It's as if we leave parts of ourselves behind when we step into a different context.

We discovered in our research that most church people do church at **church**. We do work at **work**. Even if we **think** about our faith during the week, we don't tend to **talk** about it. As in Las Vegas, what happens at church stays at church. We may want to change that! Someone wandering out in the desert of your normal workweek might love to find an oasis like your church.

A relationship with God through Christ **matters** too much to relegate it to one segment of our lives. If faith really is the most important thing in the world, mightn't it be important for a few other people too? We need to change something deep within ourselves if our faith isn't at the absolute center of our lives. Our spiritual lives can live at the center of every part of our lives, every **compartment** of our lives, every relationship, every setting, whether we say it out loud or not.

We don't need to leave church **at** church when we walk away from worship on Sunday. Church isn't the building—it's the **people**! Church is the **relationships**—our relationship with Christ, our relationships with other church members, *our relationships with people who have never thought of church or dared to walk through that door.*

This whole religious deal is so much bigger than we let it be. We tame what church can be. We **try** to tame who Christ is. For many of us, Jesus is an historical figure we "believe in." That's true, but he's also a living, risen vibrant force. He's God. If we let him, he'll be **much** more than some vaguely comforting idea in the backs of our minds. We can allow his Spirit to enter into us and work through us. If we block him from parts of our souls, from parts of our lives, he has to move around us and move on. He won't overwhelm us with fireworks. We have to open the door to him and say, "Yes."

I see a pattern in hundreds of faith-sharing stories from vastly different settings. The common denominator is that people begin to:

a. Talk about faith issues among themselves

b. Pray

c. Ask God to use them

So what would happen if we said to Jesus, "Okay. I'll pray. Will you walk with me into my life today? It's Wednesday. If your Spirit prompts me to say or do something to show your love for people, I'll do it. I'll trust you to take care of me. Use me. Please use our little group of Christians here."

What would happen if you all let Jesus use you this week to let people know how much God loves them? Of course I'm talking about doing things that are within the bounds of scripture, and theology, and accountability with a prayer partner—nothing embarrassing. I don't have any particular interest in turning into a Squirrel for Jesus. I'm moderately sure you don't either!

Connect the Dots

I *am* talking about us being willing to offer ourselves to Christ in prayer, seriously, so that God can connect all the separated parts of our lives and then use us to do some things that matter to God. Tiny changes can have large consequences. God may want you not to say a word, perhaps just to pray, watch, listen, smile. But if we pray and ask God to use us, Christ will let us know how we can be helpful to him. The Spirit can use our smallest "yes" to create miraculous, heroic, amazing, simple, loving, and powerful outcomes.

We're hearing story after story from churches in the *Unbinding the Gospel Project*. If you boil them down, the key ingredient is this: opportunities emerge when groups in the church start praying and asking God to use them to help other people learn about the faith. Here is a handful of the stories:

Story #1—The Personal Trainer: Ed is an elder in a huge Presbyterian church. He joined an *Unbinding the Gospel* study, prayer and discussion group. Ed is a life-long, active, enthusiastic church member. (One of the most frequent questions I get from life-long, active, enthusiastic church people is, "Well, how can *I* invite anyone to church? Everyone I know already *goes* to a church.") Ed's group prayed for God to use them. He began to see that not *everyone* around him had a faith community. His trainer at the gym was one. I didn't hear details, but it sounded as if the young trainer had a rather ripe vocabulary. Maybe it was the talk about girls that clued Ed into the fact that this trainer might not have a drawer full of Sunday School attendance certificates.

Ed didn't start talking. He started praying for the trainer. He had been praying every day. All of a sudden, the trainer started talking

Reese to Ted, who's 19: "I try to help people in churches pray and invite their friends to church."

Ted: "Why wouldn't they talk about Jesus and their church? How's anybody going to know if they don't *tell* them?"

with him about life issues. Now they work the free weights, figure out rep patterns, and talk about jobs, and life, and sex, and honesty, and prayer—whatever the trainer brings up as they move from one weight machine to another. Ed prays for the trainer every day. Somehow, Ed has become a safe person to talk with, sort of a big brother, or a mentor. Ed's still praying.

Story #2—"We Missed a Chance to Pray!" A pastor told me last week that the most amazing thing that has emerged from a first study of *Unbinding the Gospel* in his old New York church is a shift in awareness. Two women in the group decided to have their weekly prayer partner meeting as they hiked a paved walking path. They met a woman in a wheelchair and became engrossed in a significant conversation with her. They left the woman and continued walking. A mile down the path, one of them stopped cold and said, "We just missed an opportunity to pray with her!"

The pastor said he doubts that would have occurred to them before. He also suspects they won't miss that opportunity next time. Guess who they'll be praying for *this* week?

Story #3—"Something's changed in you." An *Unbinding* group had a long, intense discussion one week about how impossible it is to share their faith during the workweek. One teacher said, "Hey, if I talked about religion at the high school, they could fire me." Heads nodded in agreement. The pastor didn't say a word.

That week, with no prompting, friends and coworkers approached three different members of the small group with questions about faith or church. In each of the cases, the person asking the question said something like, "I guess I wouldn't have asked you this before, but something's *changed* in you."

A self-avowed atheist approached his attorney friend from the *Unbinding* group. The atheist's wife had had a baby, who was quite ill and in the hospital. The attorney listened, then said, "I know you don't believe in this, but would it be okay if I prayed for the baby?" The atheist said, "Yes. Pray if you want to."

The pastor of the church told me that "e-mails were firing around all week." The high school teacher was amazed at being asked about faith at school, the group was awed by all the comments about "Something's changed in you." The baby immediately started to get better. The attorney wrote, "I had no idea God answered prayer like that."

When We Pray, the Spirit:

Creates openness in others so that conversations "just start happening"

Opens our eyes to see opportunities

Takes the lid off our expectations of what God can do

Story #4—"We're all so close, so connected—we can tell each other anything." A Disciples of Christ congregation experienced gentle, steady decline (from 275 to 110 in average worship attendance over a 35-year period). The co-pastors have been there for six years. At the start of the *Unbinding* process, they cobbled together a young adult group made up of their daughter, her boyfriend, and two other 20-somethings in the church. They, with a great leader, started to study and pray through ***Unbinding Your Heart***. A year later, there are 25 of them.

Staci invited Jaimee, who invited Monique and about three others. Monique is married. She's bringing her three great kids, and her aunt is coming now. Jaimee went to church for a short time in fifth grade, just before her Grandpa died, but then not again until she and Jim were about to get married (that happened two months ago). I asked Jaimee what she and Jim liked about the church. She said, "People made us feel ***really*** welcomed, but nobody pressured us. They were so nice, but we didn't feel like fresh meat, like when people go, 'Oh, a young couple. We really need you. Come help our church.' But what we love is we're so close, so connected in our group.

"Nine of us got baptized at the same time. Well, just seven are in our Sunday School class, but Monique was right in front of me, and Staci was right there—we were all together in all of it. We pray together, and our prayers are being answered. We can say ***anything*** to each other. I love this church. I can look around our Sunday School room now and see 25 of us. If we hadn't invited each other, hardly anyone would be in that room. Ann, our teacher, wouldn't have a class! It's awesome that God is using us like this. Monique says, 'Sunday's my favorite day of the week.' So we just keep telling people we know how great this is."

The Spirit is moving all over that church. Average worship attendance has gone from 110 to 160 in a year, with "tons of visitors." For six weeks during Lent, 159 people studied ***Unbinding Your Heart.*** Eleven adults have been baptized this spring.

Scores of neighborhood kids are "suddenly" appearing to play at the playground basketball hoop. One of the Bible study classes decided last week to lay in a huge supply of Popsicles™, and Whiffle™ balls and bats. Seven basketball kids knocked on the door last night during board meeting, just to say hi. The pastor fished Popsicles out of the freezer. She told the kids and their mom/aunt that the church has a great band and everyone sings on Sundays too. She invited them to come to the service. One little girl started singing and said, "You've got ***music***??" The kids left finally, cellophane-wrapped VBS

"I've always been interested in spiritual issues, but never went to a church. I came to this church because I met this guy at the store. He kept the clerk from being mean to me at the Barbie display. We started talking, and he prayed that I would get the job I was interviewing for the next day. His prayers worked, and he'd invited me to his church, so that's why I came."

music CDs clutched in sweaty hands, charged with learning all the songs at home before the first Vacation Bible School meeting.

Yesterday, an 86-year-old told the pastor that she needs to invite some children who live near her to Vacation Bible School. Church people of all different ages are seeing and acting on opportunities to share their faith and to help people move into the church community. The pastor said, "Everyone's thinking this way now. It's completely different."

Nothing else in the church has changed. Same demographics. Same building. Same pastors. But they started praying and talking about their faith with each other. They asked God to use them to help new people know the joy of a conscious relationship with Christ.

The Dot-Connection, Oasis-Invitation Pattern

I see a pattern in these and the hundreds of beautiful, powerful, faith sharing stories we're hearing from vastly different settings. The common denominator is that people begin to:

(a) *talk* about faith issues among themselves

(b) *pray*

(c) *ask* God to use them

We're seeing two other dynamics:

New People: People who *didn't* grow up in the church (I'm one of them, so I have a sense of this) see the intellectual framework of Christianity, prayer, faith and a powerful Christian community as the most amazing news in the world. Whoa! Of *course* we want everyone to know about this. Obviously, we're going to tell our friends. Staci tells Jaimee, who tells Monique, who bring her kids and tells her aunt......

Church People: Church people grew up living and breathing stories about faith, and God, and prayer, and community. They often assume that everyone *knows* all this good news. They often think everyone they know *goes* to church, so they have a convenient excuse for not connecting the dots between Sunday morning at church and Wednesday evening at the ball game. BUT when churched people start to pray, the Spirit often does three things:

1. *Creates openness in our friends* or brand new acquaintances so that significant conversations "just start happening around me" (Friends perceive it as, "something in you has changed.")

2. *Opens our eyes so we can see* the opportunities, opens our ears so we hear the tones of voice and the subtext of conversations

As we went to print, the pastor of the story #4 church sent me an e-mail:

"We ended up with 92 kids attending VBS!! And we had 56 church members helping! Wow! Two people joined the church yesterday. God has really touched all our lives. It was a great day of rejoicing."

we're part of (Ed and the trainer & "We missed an opportunity to pray!")

> *3. **Takes the lid off our expectations*** of what God can do ("I had no idea God answered prayer like that.")

We cannot imagine what God can do with our lives if we'll ask and be open. There may be thousands of tiny ways God can use ***each*** of us, and ***groups*** of us, during the rest of our lives. We probably won't even be aware God's using us as some of these things happen. But God ***will*** be aware. So will the people whose lives change.

Look carefully at all the people you see as you go through your day today. Try to see them the way they felt in high school. Does that sales manager unconsciously feel like the nerdy guy eating lunch at the jock's table? Can your elegant, middle-aged neighbor in Chanel dress and Manolo Blahnik shoes still look in the mirror and see the lumpy, frumpy 15-year-old who wouldn't dare try out for the cheerleading squad? Would the nerd and the frump (and the two perfectly normal adults they've grown into) like a place where they can be loved for themselves, where they can do something for other people?

Wouldn't you love to know them better? Maybe they'd like a place in this ***Unbinding Your Soul*** group, where they can talk about their lives, for real? We ***all*** need that!

Can you connect your Sunday with your Monday? …your Thursday? People outside the oasis need you to try. People ***inside*** the oasis need you to try!

We need to change something deep within ourselves if our faith isn't at the absolute center of our lives. Our spiritual lives can live at the center of every part of our lives, every ***compartment*** of our lives, every relationship, every setting, whether we say it out loud or not.

GROUP DISCUSSION_____

1. Begin your group time with Prayer Triads (see page 41).

2. What has God done during your prayer times this week? What are you wondering about?

3. How connected are the different parts of your life? How do you behave differently in the various arenas you enter? (What were your quiz results on Day 2 this week?)

4. Can you think of one specific way you might grow to help connect your spiritual life with your "normal" life?

GROUP EXERCISE _____

(Take about half your group time to do this)

Divide into groups of three. Sit quietly for a couple of minutes and think about/ask God:

- "What do I love best about this church and this group of people?"

Take a couple of minutes each to talk about it. Now sit quietly again for two minutes. Ask God to show you:

- Whom do I know in my life outside church who would appreciate what I've found here?
- Whom do I know who might need a group like this right now?
- Whom do I know who would add a lot to our discussion and prayer?

(Jot down notes as ideas come to you. Think of powerful people who have strong ideas and opinions. Think of quiet people whom you suspect could teach you a lot.)

Talk with two other people about what you perceived during the silence. Then combine into the full group and continue the discussion.

Are you called to go forward? Discuss whether you sense as a group that God is calling you to invite friends to form a new group in a couple of weeks. What has happened as you have prayed with the fresh copies of ***Unbinding Your Soul*** during your prayer times this week? Don't think now about whether you, individually, can "get" someone to come into the group. That's not the question.

Look at what you all sense the Spirit is nudging you to do. You may know already. If you aren't sure, maybe these questions could help you get clearer:

1. Is this a good group? Does it help you?

2. Is it a safe place to talk about substantial faith issues? ***Are*** you talking about substantial life and faith issues?

3. Might this group and process help other people? Think specifically about the people who came to mind during the silence just now.

4. Are ***you*** open to hearing spiritual ideas and opinions that may be very different from yours? Life-long church people can get some big shocks talking with people who don't drag themselves

We need to get over the idea that the church is the "dispenser of information and correct ideas." If the church is truly to be a spiritual community, inviting to all, we'll spend ***much*** more time listening to people who don't go to church, ***occasionally*** saying what we believe, and almost ***no*** time telling them what they're supposed to think. It's God who changes minds. Are ***you*** brave enough to stand back and let the Spirit work?

out of bed on Sunday mornings, but who read the paper or go on long runs, or to the deli. We need to get over the idea that the church is the "dispenser of information and correct ideas." If the church is truly to be a spiritual community, inviting to all, we'll spend **much** more time listening to people who don't go to church, occasionally saying what we believe, and almost **no** time telling them what they're supposed to think. It's God who changes our minds. Are **you** brave enough to stand back and let the Spirit work?

Pray Together: After you've discussed this, you may know whether you should invite friends into the group. Pray about it and for your friends now.

Review Appendix to Chapter 7 as a group: What do you think? Questions? Ideas?

Don't worry about results. That's up to the Spirit. Please don't worry about whether a person you invite says, "yes." I know one of you is worrying that you'll be the only person who won't have a friend join the group. Okay—say it out loud—who's thinking that??

Let it go! Just let your friend have the choice of whether to accept or not. Some of you may be called to ask two or three people into a new group that will start Part One in a couple of weeks. Some people may say no, but someone else may pop into your mind. Let the Spirit take care of who accepts, okay? Just keep praying the book will find its owner! (You may need to give out a couple of books—someone could take a copy, keep it, say "no" to The Experiment Group, and read the book anyway. They might join a second round, later. You never know what's going to happen!)

Your Group's Foundations:

- Speak honestly.
- Speak and listen in love.
- Explore new ideas.
- Maintain confidentiality

ASSIGNMENT FOR THE WEEK _____

Read the Appendix to chapter 7. Do it!

Appendix to Chapter 7

Invite Your Friend to Be in The Experiment Group with You

1. Read the Introduction. Reread the introduction to **Unbinding Your Soul** on pages xi to xiii to see what you're inviting your friend to do.

2. Pray again. Ask God/Christ/the Spirit to let you know clearly if God would really like you to invite a friend into the group. If not, don't worry about it! Maybe your job is to pray for other people's invitations. Just ask God and see.

3. Ask God whom to invite. If you get a sense of "yes" from God, ask God: "Whom should I invite into this group? From whom do we need to hear? Who can help me learn what you want me to learn next? Which of my friends might love this group and this experience?" It could be someone you don't know well. The person may have lived next door to you for 20 years. You might have thought of them two weeks ago, or God may show you someone who had never popped into your mind before. (It could be two or three people!)

4. Ask how to invite. Sit in silence for a bit and ask God how to invite the person. Do you have a sense of that person's interests? Needs? Next steps of growth? Pray for them. You might want to call your prayer partner and ask him/her to pray with you. Now take whatever next step you sense would be helpful. Call the person you feel prompted to invite into the group.

5. Take the next step. Invite them to lunch or coffee. Go over to their house.

6. Listen. Ask how they are. Listen. Do you remember at the end of chapter 5, when you listened to two other people tell a story of God in their lives and you prayed for them as they talked? Do that now. Listen to the person you're going to invite.

7. Explain and invite. Here are topics it might be helpful to discuss with your friend:

- Describe a bit about how this last three weeks of the group has been for you—about the group, what the people are like, the experience of talking about your lives and experimenting with different types of prayers.

- Explain that the group has decided to go on to new material, and you've each decided you'd like to invite in one friend who has really interesting ideas and who might love this group of people.

- The new group will meet for four weeks to talk about important life and faith issues and to experiment with different classic Christian prayer disciplines.

- It will include people who are interested in spiritual issues, some of whom may think of themselves as Christians, many of whom may not. The group wants to include wide-open discussion and varied perspectives.

- Let them know that they are the friend with whom *you'd* love to do this.

- Don't ask for an answer right away. Give them a copy of **Unbinding Your Soul,** ask them to read the Introduction and chapter 1 to get a sense of what it's like.

■ Give them a chance to think and pray about it, but let them know how much you'd love them to be part of this four-week experiment/adventure.

8. *See what happens!* If s/he says yes, you can serve as this person's prayer partner and buddy during the next four weeks. You can keep in touch with them during the week, pick them up and drive them to the first meeting. (It's best to have these meetings in someone's home.) Walk with your friend through this amazing month! See what God can do with both of you and the whole group. (You and your current prayer partner can still connect each week to talk, and to pray for the group and the friends you've invited into it.)

Notes

What Does a Spiritual Life Look Like?

Scripture: Galatians 5:16–26

Get settled to pray. Relax. Read this scripture slowly. Which words and phrases seem most important to you? Mark them in your Bible or write them down.

Paul gives us two pretty different lists here, doesn't he? Wow! This whole "works of the flesh," "fruit of the Spirit" thing is dramatic. What's Paul talking about? It's important to understand. This is one of the huge points of Christianity. Paul says that we humans naturally tend to be self-centered and focused on instant gratification. Our normal inclination is to eat the chocolate chip cookie, grump at your family, take the money when no one's looking, drink too much, have the affair, fight, manipulate and to let jealousy corrode your soul like battery acid (verses 19–21).

But Paul tells the Galatians (and us) that saying "yes" to Christ—asking God to enter into our lives and heal us from this stuff—actually makes a difference in who we are, in how we instinctively respond to situations. The Holy Spirit can change us from the inside. We will begin to see changes in how we think and act (verses 22–25). We get better.

Reread the passage. Where do *you* fall in these two lists? Think over the last week. Ask God to show you the moments when you were closest to life in the flesh, and the moments when your life actually demonstrated fruits of the Spirit.

Do you want to ask God to take over more of your life, transform you more? Do it.

Notes, lists, insights:

I'm praying for:_____

Insight: "It's a feeling that goes between the marrow and the bones….Sometimes I want to fly away. I feel like I have something deep inside of me. It's a charge to glorify Him in preaching and singing." *Mother Willie Mae Ford Smith, 20th Century, American Gospel Singer*

Repentance

Scripture: Matthew 3:1–12

Light your candle. Relax. Read about John the Baptist.

I have a hard time reading scriptures that talk about repentance and winnowing forks and chaff being burned with unquenchable fire. I'd much rather read nice things.

However, I am a pretty mixed bag. I live with great gifts and abilities, mixed with selfish impulses, competitiveness, old moldy habits and damage, and some very beautiful parts of my character that the Holy Spirit is growing in me. Everything's mixed up together inside me, so maybe a little separating and winnowing and burning isn't such a horrible idea!

A wise friend told me years ago, "You're going to have to repent of everything anyone's ever done to you." !!!!! I thought, "Oh, *yeah*, I'm certainly going to give up *my* professional victim status!" But she kept talking. I finally realized she *wasn't* telling me that I was responsible for, or had caused, or had to repent for other people's bad actions (sins). She *was* saying that if I *judge* someone for harming me, if I *resent* them and don't let go of it, my resentments or judgments anchor *their* sins to *my* soul with spiritual fishhooks!

So I asked God to show me anything I needed to let go of, anything of which I needed to repent. For the next few days I got little flashes of memories. Most of them were little, tiny things I hadn't thought about in years. Lots of them were nothing you'd ever think of as a sin. (Some were.) Each time one of these little pictures came into my mind, I said, "God, help me to hand this to you. I'm sorry for being resentful, or petty, or bitter. Please heal this in me."

I have never been quite the same. That week of prayer proved to be a pivot point in my life. I still can't explain it. It didn't feel as if God were healing open wounds. It felt as if God were removing old, internal scar tissue. It might help you to do something similar. I invite you to ask God to show you if there's anything of which you could repent. If something flickers into your mind, hand it to God.

Notes, drawings, thoughts, insights:

Prayer: God, I want to repent of anything that's keeping me from being whole and completely usable by you. Please heal me. Show me the old memories, wounds, sins, bitterness or judgments that are taking up space in my soul. Help me to hand them to you. Thank you, God! I want to trust that you can heal me. Will you? Amen.

A Prayer Walk Through *Your* House

Scripture: Mark 6:1–6; Acts 18:5–11

As a guest speaker, I've asked thousands of people to talk about their faith and to pray with total strangers. Almost everyone says the same thing, "This was **great**! But it would be a lot harder to do this in my **own** church, with all the people I've wrestled with over the budget for 20 years." Yep. Probably.

Want to raise the scariness factor to pole vault level? Think about talking about faith and prayer with your own *family*. I hear you! Are you thinking, "Maybe I should leave well enough alone? At least Ed will come to church four or five times a year, and I can maneuver the kids into youth group most of the time." Read the scriptures for today. Even Jesus had trouble in *his* hometown! But look at the passage from the book of Acts. Crispus "became a believer in the Lord, ***together with all his household.***" Okay. It was probably easier in days when dads just told people what to do and everyone did it. Maybe.

But I think we can do more to encourage faith in our families than most of us do.

Would you start by walking through your house, room-by-room, praying for your family? Pray for the kids in their rooms. (If you *are* a kid, pray for the other kids' rooms, your parents' room.) Put your hand on the headboard of the beds, on their laptops, and think or say, "Jesus, please let her open her mind to you when she touches her desk." Bless your own closet and dresser ("Lord, please clothe me in righteousness"). Bless the dining room ("Please, Lord, let our meals be like dinner with you"). Touch doorframes ("Bless each one who walks through this door"), the furnace ("Warm us with your love"). Imagine each family member in their favorite seat and pray, "Holy Spirit, live between us and help us love you and each other more."

Now, pray for the home of the person you're inviting into your faith group. Go through the rooms in your imagination and bless them just as you blessed your own house. "See" their home and "walk" through the rooms, one at a time, praying. Then visit. Or call. Or invite them to your house. Pray about it.

Notes, drawings, thoughts:

*I'm praying for:*_____

Prayer: God, let our home become a place where you live. Please change us. Turn us into the family only you can make us. Thank you, God. Amen.

The Still, Small Voice

Scripture: 1 Kings 19:9–18

Light your candle. Relax. Read this story about the prophet Elijah. What strikes you as important? Read it again. Pay particular attention to verses 11–13.

God spoke to Elijah. Isn't it curious that God doesn't blow in on the wind, as the wind tears up mountains? God doesn't speak to Elijah out of the wind, or the earthquake, or the fire. Instead, after a time of sheer silence (in some translations, "a still, small voice," or "a soft, whispering murmur") God speaks.

Here's a truth about God—God could blast and do earthquakes to get our attention, but very often God shows Godself very quietly. This is one of the reasons we pray. Prayer isn't just talking to God. Prayer can be sitting and listening. Thomas Keating, a great teacher of prayer, says that as we get older and more used to God, we don't need so many words any more. Christians who have prayed for years often sit silently in prayer for long stretches of time, without saying or thinking anything. Keating says we can get to the point in our prayer lives where we sit with God like two old married people on a porch. They don't say anything for hours, just sit and occasionally touch the other one's hand.

Will you just sit with God for a while today? Breathe slowly. Tell God that you want to just sit with him. Don't worry when random thoughts about grocery lists or your geometry test at school pop into your head. Pretend the thoughts are like a stick on a river and you're sitting on the bank. Just let the thoughts drift past. Just sit with God.

Notes, drawings, thoughts:

*I'm praying for:*_____

Prayer: Thank you, God, that I can just *be* with you and don't need to have the "right" words. Amen.

Just Talk with Your Prayer Partner!

You're great! Congratulations. What an intense three weeks of prayer you've finished! How has this week been?? Would you like a day to thank God, to relax a bit? Why don't you meet with your prayer partner and talk about everything. How did this week affect you? What happened? What did you do? What thoughts did you have? What did you learn? How did you grow close to God?

How is your prayer for each other going? How are those situations in your lives? Talk about what it has been like to pray together for others. Do you need to refocus those prayers? Pray together and thank God for this time. Pray for the people you're each inviting into the group. If you haven't invited them yet, find out when your prayer partner is going to talk with their friend and pray for them now, before and at that time.

Notes, drawings, lists, thoughts:

*Prayer for:*_____

Reflection Day

Read. Have you read chapter 8 so you're ready for tomorrow's group meeting?

Review. Think back over your week of prayer. Reread your favorite scripture. Review your notes, lists, insights. How is your prayer going?

Then, answer two questions:

Question 1: What are the most important things you've learned/discovered/remembered this week?

Question 2: What one insight would God like me to share with my study group when we meet?

*Prayer for:*_____

Prayer: Talk to God. Sit in silence. Listen. Amen.

A pastor's prayer life...

Coach to pastors, "Do you see signs of transformation in your churches as a result of the *Unbinding the Gospel* process?" One pastor described three changes in church leadership, meetings and dynamics. Then he said:

"And I humbly add, the old saying 'speed of the leader, speed of the team' comes into play on this issue. As I pray with greater consistency and openness, and as I listen in various ways for God's interactions, I sense personal, spiritual transformation. I have begun a weekly discipline—Saturday mornings usually—prayerfully visiting with God about the nine fruits of the Spirit Paul lifts up. [Galatians 5:16-26, remember from Week F, Day 1?] It's an interactive conversation in which I pose the question: 'God, how is your Spirit growing love in me?' Then I let my mind be open to experiences from the past week that God brings to my remembrance: the person who entered the church needing assistance and the absence of a spirit of judgmentalism I felt.

Then I asked, 'God, how is your Spirit growing joy in me?' To my mind came the encounters I had experienced with my own grandchildren, how they rushed to me with beaming smiles on their faces and jumped into my arms. God helped me understand in my reflection on those moments that I need to receive unconditional love as well as offer it to others. In that receiving, I knew immense joy.

Working through those manifestations of God's faithful work in me have helped me to realize God is near, God's Spirit is truly responsible for the growth, and more is happening in the spiritual growth of my life and of others than I had been observing before. This awareness of God is transforming my prayer life.

Failing to go to God in prayer impedes my progress. Allowing other people's negativity to be the last word impedes the transformation the good news brings. With the growing sense that God will indeed do great things through us, I expect we will become less prone to give in to impediments."

CHAPTER 8

What Keeps Me on Shore?

Two men waved good-bye to their families in Copenhagen and boarded a ship for a cruise to the West Indies. One's wife and children were in tears, begging him not to go, but John Leonard Dober and David Nitschman, a potter and a carpenter, continued up the gangplank. Actually, it wasn't exactly a cruise like the Princess Cruises to the Caribbean. Dober and Nitschman were Moravians. It was 1732. They were heading to the West Indies to sell themselves into slavery so they could preach to the slaves.

Don't try this at home, boys and girls.

Or maybe this is *exactly* the type of faith we should try at home! This story of the first Moravian missionaries inspired John Wesley, whose ministry launched the Methodists and fueled the Great Awakening—a giant revival that rolled throughout New England for decades in the 1700s.

I don't believe that heroic stories belong only in the past. *We* belong to the same God—God can use us too. Our stories may be humble, but we never know what God can do with our smallest efforts to obey.

I know one thing. The story of Dober and Nitschman selling themselves into slavery out of love for Christ and their love for other people puts my pitiful anxieties, fears, prides and grumpiness into perspective! I'd better just get over that stuff!

The things that keep me from following Christ wholeheartedly amaze me. Laziness holds me back. Prayer disciplines infuse me with the reality and the power of God's love for me. But it's hard to get up at 5:30 some mornings.

"I kept hearing all the objections to doing the *Unbinding the Gospel* study. 'We don't have time.' 'It's too much commitment.' 'It's too hard.' 'No one will do it.' 'We don't want the church to change.' 'We don't *want* new people.' I thought and thought about it. I finally realized I was afraid and that being afraid unsettled me and made me mad. I wasn't afraid it would change the church. I was afraid it would change *me*."

A six-year-old appeared at my friend's door on Halloween. She was dressed in a big, black trash bag that had yellow sponges glued all over it. Karen asked, "Are you Sponge-Bob Square Pants?" The little girl answered, "No, I'm self-absorbed."

Sometimes I'm just afraid. I don't want the Spirit to disturb my comfortable life. Or I'm selfish. I'd rather not hand over time, or money, or change my habits.

Also, I really *like* being in control of my own life.

I assume I can figure things out for myself, thank you very much. To rely on God isn't *my* default position.

Jacqueline Solem is an artist, a therapist and a spiritual director in northern Minnesota. She says that one of three things stops most of us from growing: fear, anger or pride. Think of that: most of us have a "preferred" mode of being stopped from following God! Look at the list of things a group of Methodists answered when their pastor asked what scared them about doing an E-vent, an all-church, small group study of **Unbinding Your Heart**. *(See opposite page. Then, if you want to see how it all turned out, read p. 156–158.)*

As I read that list, I think I see a "pride" and an "anger" reaction, in addition to all the "fear" responses that the pastor asked about. Take a look and see if you spot two answers that look a little different.

"Our 72 small group facilitators for our E-vent met in training sessions last week. They were great. We've never done anything like this all-church study at First Church. I really appreciate their honesty and transparency. I asked them to just call out what they were afraid of. Here's a condensed list of their answers:

It might change our church

I may not be able to stick with it—huge commitment

No one will sign up for MY group

I'm afraid of gossip, breaking of confidentiality

Fear of judgment, criticism, and therefore the fear of sharing

We might become like a Catholic church *(MGR note—other churches add the following list of fears: We might become like evangelicals...liberals...Pentecostals)*

I'm afraid of anything different or new

I don't know enough

I'm afraid of being rejected

I'm horrified of evangelism

I've never been involved in a small group with strangers (uncomfortable)

We like the church the way it is—we're afraid to grow.

It's intimidating to ask everyone to read a book

Am I good enough to do this?

I'm afraid people will be embarrassed if others see they don't have personal faith.

I can't just be a spectator in a small group

Will I have to read out loud or pray out loud?

I'm OK. I don't need it.

I'm not going to do what everybody is doing just because they are doing it.

It might change me

We prayed in groups of three. Then I asked if their level of fear was higher or lower than it was at the beginning of the meeting. It was unanimously LOWER. Unexpectedly, people discovered that when you invite God to enter your space, perfect love really does cast out fear. (1 John 4:18)*

---

*E-mail to Reese from a United Methodist pastor, leading his large church through the **Unbinding the Gospel/Unbinding Your Heart** process.

These are typical fears, particularly halfway through the **GOSPEL/HEART** process. If you want to see what God and these people did by the end, see Roger Ross, "An Unbinding Focus," pages 156–158.

You can pretend you're a seven-year old at a restaurant, looking for the answers in upside-down type at the bottom of the kid's puzzle placemat, elbowing your brother as you wait for your pancakes to arrive. Mark the answers that aren't the same with one of your crayons.☺ The two responses I think are motivated by pride or anger appear in a footnote at the bottom of this page.**

Okay. Let's get serious here. What's *your* typical, first reaction to a new challenge or a new idea? How does *your* voice sound in *your* head?

- "Oh, I'm afraid _____ will happen." (Fear—look at all the things the Methodists said they were afraid of. Those are typical fears.)

- "That's inappropriate. It's certainly not the right way to do it." (Pride)

- "I absolutely will not…. Rant….. rant….. rant…. growl, growl, growl all the way home." (That would be anger)

If you aren't clear which typical emotional response rears its ugly head as you react to challenges, you might ask your family. We can be amazingly unconscious about ourselves, but our families usually have a pretty good bead on us! Just know that when you

feel like running away and *hiding*,
or you think you know better and these people are *wrong*,
or you get really *ticked off* with the utter ridiculousness of some new idea,

it doesn't mean you shouldn't do it! Our initial reactions serve only as an emotional *signal* that something new is ahead. We'll want to sit with the idea for a while, talk with some people, and *then* make a conscious choice about whether it's a good idea. A knee-jerk "no" may not be our most faith-filled response!

Where the Rubber Meets the Road

Let's apply these ideas to a practical situation that may help you see how you operate in the rest of your life. How did you respond to the idea of inviting friends into The Experiment Group? Was it exciting?

> "It is an amazing story of God leading all of us – most particularly me – into places none of us thought possible even a year ago! We are running on legs of fear and awe."
>
> —*a Presbyterian pastor*

** I think these two answers look different: "I'm OK. I don't need it." (Pride?), and "I'm not going to do what everybody is doing just because they are doing it." (You'd have to hear the tone of voice, but perhaps that's an anger response? Maybe it's pride.)

Where do you sense resistance in yourself? Did your group decide to invite friends into an Experiment Group for a "second half" study of Part One? How did you feel about the decision? Have you been praying? Here's the $40,000 question: Have you invited someone?

If you **have** already invited someone, how did you feel? Take the quiz:

❑ Easy! I did it. It was great!

❑ I did it, but it felt as if I were

  ❑ teeing off at the U.S. Open

  ❑ standing up to play my piece at the piano recital

❑ It started scary, but the conversation was amazing!

❑ Couldn't quite get there

If you "couldn't quite get there," and want to take another run at it, why don't you reread the appendix to chapter 7, page 101. That may help. Ask God if you should take another shot at it. There's more time before The Experiment Group starts. But this is only an example that may help you see a little more about yourself, not the main point. Don't worry about the invitation. Please! Just offer the whole thing to God and ask God's direction. God adores you—don't let there be pressure, "oughts" or "shoulds" in your head!

Heroes and Heroines & Little Tiny Steps

I realized something important about myself as I have been writing and rewriting this book for you. Bear with this detour, will you?

Aunt Phoebe is Dad's sister—one of Grandmother and Grandad Reese's two incredible daughters. She gave me the *Good Housekeeping's Best Book of Heroes and Heroines* for Christmas in 5th grade.[1] I must have read it 10 or 15 times. Memories of my feelings as I read specific chapters as a girl have cropped up during the last month. I keep thinking about reading chapters about Joan of Arc, Madam Curie, Albert Schweitzer, Father Damian and Walter Reed.

I've realized that this book formed me—with all those **other** heroic books, and movies, and family stories of my childhood. Part of me will probably always respond to heroes—to Pheidippides dying after he ran 26 miles from Marathon to Athens to announce the news of the great Greek victory, to the idea of surrendering self in the service of people you don't even know. A deep part of me wants to offer my

"I led an Advent study. Only 7 people showed up....7! All I could think was.... 'Oh my, the first initiative since I arrived and it may fail.' I freaked out so much the week before the sign-ups for **Unbinding Your Heart,** I got on my knees and said, 'It's up to you, God.' Okay, here's an admission – I never do that. I prayed we could get 88 folks – we now have 132 who have remained with the experience. They're so excited and engaged. They're interviewing friends from work. This is changing lives!"

—pastor (This Midwest church has gone from 95 to 195 in worship attendance in one year.)

life up for something way more important than my individual self. My life won't last forever. I want to leave it all out on the field.

That's probably what makes me respond so strongly to the story of the two Moravians setting sail for the West Indies—to sell themselves into slavery so they could tell the slaves about Jesus. They left it all out on the field.

Don't let my heroics, rooted in my past, make you feel as if I'm trying to run up that gangplank and drag *you* with me! The point is, nobody needs to follow my example—we're all quirky in specific ways.

So, let me say this more gently, less heroically.

God loves us overwhelmingly. God loves everyone else in the world too—in ways too profound for us to understand. When we say "yes" to Jesus, to God, to the Spirit, we're somehow signing on to be with God, as God loves and cares for all these people, for all of creation.

God will patiently, lovingly, bring us along. God will help us heal and mature. God will help us move into caring for others. Even the heroes and heroines in the Good Housekeeping book took little, tiny steps. Huge results come from thousands of tiny decisions, routine work, weeks and months of just going along. Bill Gates is supposed to have said that most people overestimate what can be done in a year and underestimate what can happen in 10 years.

We don't need to worry about heroism, or ultimate results of our efforts. We won't know those things. We just need to take whatever next small step God would like us to take.

My friend Nikki MacMillan thinks Jesus helps us follow him the way parents help a kid learn to swim. As a child, you look across the huge swimming pool and know you can't swim!! Your mom gets right in front of you, *just* out of reach, and you swim toward her—one dog paddle, three kicks, you keep pedaling and paddling. Your mom moves imperceptibly backwards, grins, and tells you how great you are! You keep kicking and pushing down with your arms to keep your head up. You don't even *realize* how far you're going. Good job!

Nikki's right. That's how God is with us. All we need to do is concentrate on Jesus—he's holding out his arms to you, telling you how wonderful you are and how great you're doing. All you have to do is follow step, by step, by step. God will take care of the outcomes.

Here's the main point. We can learn to love Christ and follow him, not merely "believe in" him. How? Tell Jesus you want to love him and know him. Ask him to give you a hand so that you can get

> "I know God is preparing us for something wonderful. I know He is faithful, and if we are faithful to His call, he will bless us beyond anything we can today imagine. If anyone dared to suggest a year ago that I would be willing to step out as a layman and lead our church in evangelism, I would have asked them if they were smoking dope! Today I believe that we should strap on our seatbelts and get ready for the ride of a lifetime!"
>
> —*a Disciples of Christ elder*

into the pool and learn to dog-paddle. We can pray, worship, read scripture, and talk honestly with other dear people who are trying to let God use them, too. Pray every day. Ask God to use us. It's not rocket science. It's spiritual habits.

The Spirit can help us change (be braver, humbler, more joyful/ less angry, faithful, gentle, patient, loving) if we'll practice, if we'll start taking little steps. Want to play the piano? Practice! Want to be an accountant? Do the exercises every day. It's cumulative. Want to be a Christian God can work through? Pray! Offer God the next hour of your life. Ask God today to bless you and teach you and work through you. Work with a group of people who are also stumbling along God's path.

None of us is particularly impressive, but God can do amazing things with us if we'll ask what God would like us to do, and then ask God to give us the courage to do it!

We don't have any idea what God could do with our lives if we would offer ourselves to God without reservations attached. Do you remember the quote that opened chapter 8? (on page 110). A pastor prayed to ask God to help him see how the Holy Spirit was growing the qualities Paul calls the "gifts of the Spirit" in him. Will serves a large church filled with wonderful people in a beautiful neighborhood in a big Midwestern city. He and his church took the ***Unbinding the Gospel/Heart*** all-church study very seriously (and joyously). They prayed alone in their homes. They talked about the ideas in the books for hours. They prayed together when they met.

I asked Will what came out of it all. He told me that he has changed. The experience is joy-filled, and it's real, but it isn't easy. The church is enlivened, and they're praying. They're working on significant new ministries in the neighborhood and the city. He says he's vividly aware of a neighborhood three blocks away from the church that he had driven past for five years, but never actually ***seen***.

Suddenly homeless people and people who have spent years in prison are showing up at the church. He's talking with them, brother to brother. They have asked to be baptized. The day Will and I spoke, he had received text messages from a man who was on the run from a drug-dealer's contract on his life. An entirely new world was opening up, and lawyers and politicians in the congregation were giving Will advice. They're beginning to mobilize wisdom and resources to help. Will has no idea where it's all going. It's too new. But he identifies all

> We don't have to be perfect. We don't have to know what we're doing. We don't have to know where we're going, how we'll get there, or what results God is going to bring out of it. God will handle that. All we have to do is be available and obedient, pretty much of the time. God will take care of the rest. Will you say yes?

of these events—the enlivening of the congregation, the new spirit of peace and adventure, his new ability to see a world he'd been living next to for years—as the work of the Spirit.

"I knew these things could happen. I've felt close to God for most of my life. But this feels different. It is hard, and it feels dangerous. I believe it's exactly where God wants me to be."

"I baptized a married couple last week and will baptize a young mother on Sunday. We have an influx of young couples visiting the church right now, and it feels so good. With God's presence, we are following fire and clouds on a journey to wholeness."

Most people who know the story of John Leonard Dober and David Nitschman talk about their bravery and love of Christ. They talk about something else too. The Moravian Community of Herrnhut in Saxony (modern Germany) began an around-the-clock "prayer watch" five years before those two men boarded the ship for the West Indies. This prayer vigil continued non-stop for over 100 years. Dober and Nitschman were only the first missionaries who went to serve the least and the lost for whom the community was praying. Within 65 years, this small community sent over 300 missionaries to some of the poorest, most remote, undiscovered and abandoned places in the world.

God can use us all. It's better if we pray. All we have to do is pray and follow Jesus, be responsive to the Spirit in the next step. God may call you to do a mission trip, or to make an apology, to plant 100 trees, or to see Jesus in the face of a boy with Down's Syndrome. God may be calling you to try a new way of relating to your spouse, to help build an orphanage for AIDS orphans, to send someone a note, to have tea with a friend.

We don't need to worry about heroism, or ultimate results of our efforts. We won't know those things. We just need to take whatever next small step God would like us to take.

We don't have to be perfect. We don't have to know what we're doing. We don't have to know where we're going, how we'll get there, or what results God is going to bring out of it.

God will handle all *those* parts of it. All we have to do is be available and obedient. God will take care of the rest. Will you say "yes?"

---

[1]Pauline Rush Evans, *Good Housekeeping's Best Book of Heroes and Heroines* (Englewood Cliffs, N.J.: Prentice Hall, 1958).

GROUP DISCUSSION

1. Begin with Prayer Triads (page 41).

2. What happened in connection with your prayer this week?

3. What do you think of the story of the Moravians selling themselves into slavery so they could preach to the slaves? Have you ever felt you were following God? Did you recognize it at the time, or in hindsight? What tends to stop you from responding to God? (Fear? Anger? Pride?)

GROUP EXERCISE

Divide into groups of Three.

Sit quietly in silence for two minutes and ask God to help you see the real answer to this question:

"God, are there some little steps you'd like me to take now?"

Take a couple of minutes each to talk about it.

Pray & Discuss

How have your invitations into The Experiment Group gone so far? Do you need to plan more for your first Experiment Group meeting—more invitations? ...follow-up phone calls? ...group division to keep the group at 8-10? ...meeting place logistics?

Pray together as a group for each of the new people who will be joining you next week. Ask God to bless them. Ask the Spirit to show you any ways you can be more welcoming and help the experience be as normal and comfortable for them as possible.

Ask God if there's someone new the Spirit is prompting you to ask during this "in between" week. Do it! Pray for each other and the friends you're going to invite in the week to come.

ENDING THIS GROUP

This is the last meeting of your original group. Spend two or three minutes in silence, inviting the group to think about the gifts each group member has contributed to these times together. Go around the circle and let two or three people describe in one sentence what great gift each person in the group has brought. For example, "I'm so grateful for John's honesty and encouragement—he keeps showing me how to speak the truth in a kind way."

> The Spirit can help us change (be braver, humbler, more joyful/ less angry, faithful, gentle, patient, loving) if we'll practice, if we'll start taking little steps. Want to play the piano? Practice! Want to be an accountant? Do the exercises every day. It's cumulative.

Close in Prayer

Close the group with prayer. You could put a hand on each person's shoulder or arm as you pray for God's blessings, your thankfulness for their lives. Then pray by name for each person you're inviting into the group next week. End with the Lord's Prayer, prayed in unison.

ASSIGNMENT FOR NEXT WEEK _____

Read the introduction and chapter 1 of this book in preparation for next week's first meeting of the new group. There are no prayer exercises for this week. Pray on your own. Will you repeat the exercises we've already done? Read scripture the way we have on Mondays (it's called "lexio divina," sacred reading). Repeat favorite readings, or choose other scripture passages. Pray in silence. Pray for a neighborhood. Experiment, using the last three weeks' exercises as a model.

Please pray each day for the group and for the people joining it next week. Stay in touch with the person you've invited into the group. Stay encouraged. Call a couple of days before the first meeting. Make sure they've read:

- The introduction to *Unbinding Your Soul*
- Chapter 1, **and**
- *Using Your Prayer Journal*

See how they liked it. Pick up your friend and go together to the first meeting. Perhaps you could have dinner, lunch or coffee first.

Blessings upon you as you move through this amazing "in between" week!

Want to be a Christian God can work through? Pray! Offer God the next hour of your life. Ask God today to bless you and teach you and work through you. Work with a group of people who are also stumbling along God's path!

Unbinding Your Soul

PART THREE | # Resources to Help with the Unbinding...

■ **PART ONE**
The Experiment in Prayer & Community

■ **PART TWO**
Faith & Courage

■ **PART THREE**
Resources to Help with the Unbinding

- Using Your Prayer Journal
- Facilitators' & Pastors' Guides
- Next Steps

I have heard of your faith in the Lord Jesus and your love toward all the saints, and for this reason I do not cease to give thanks for you as I remember you in my prayers.
Ephesians 1:15-16

When we pray...

"I can't believe this, but prayer and the Great Commission [Matthew 28:18-20] are beginning to rival duck hunting on my list of priorities."

—a Minnesotan

"We started the prayer journal last week. I must admit, setting aside intentional time to pray is hard for me. But I understand that it is essential to a powerful life with God at the center. I have ADHD, and it's hard for me to focus, so I appreciate the prayers where you walk around or do things. Those are actually pretty awesome."

[Full text of a second e-mail from this man seven weeks later]: "Thank you for making us all pray. God's doing amazing things here—not only in the church, but in my family."

—a pastor

"God's nudges are becoming more frequent as I become more willing to pay attention."

—a pastor

"My little sister got really upset when I was baby-sitting for her. I remembered that prayer we did about Peace a couple of weeks ago. So I said, 'Why don't we do that prayer again?' and we did. We sat on the couch and we each prayed that Jesus would be holding each of us and that we'd feel him there and calm down. Then we prayed for some friends of ours—like we were sitting on Jesus' lap and we were holding different friends on our laps. Ashley stopped crying and felt better. I felt much more peaceful too. It was really good to remember that I can pray when things aren't so good."

—an eighth grader

CHAPTER 9

Using Your Prayer Journal

I love praying. It's my lifeline to God. But I'm also a multitasking workaholic. I have discovered, over the course of an eventful life, that my dog-with-a-bone, worker-bee ethic makes me want to ignore prayer. I'm also discovering (slowly, ever so slowly) that prayer is the only effective antidote to my deep-seated sense that it's the tension in my jaw that keeps the world turning. Prayer, reading scripture and talking with people about faith remind me that *I'm* not God, that *God* is God. I'm allowed to help.

God reminds me, gently, or with the occasional 2 x 4 upside the head, that God's majesty and glory are all that really matters in the world. I can rest in God. In God, in Christ, my life has infinite meaning. Not so much when I'm off on my own!

Praying consistently isn't easy. I swoop eagle-like on currents of glorious inspiration—every once in a while. But many days I'd rather talk than pray, read than pray, sleep than pray. Gosh, I'd rather organize the garage some days. I possess impressive avoidance mechanisms to shield myself from going face-to-Face with God. Yet I *have* developed a daily prayer discipline.

I've learned not to wait to brush my teeth until I am moved by a spontaneous burst of creativity. I don't wait to exercise until I am smitten with a wild desire to lift the dreaded weights! It's pretty much the same with prayer. I've learned that my life is better if I pray every day. Other people's lives are better if I pray every day. So at 5:30 almost every morning, we're up praying at our house. On the other days, I pray when I take long walks or paddle my kayak (or lift weights). So if you have tendencies to think, "I'll pray in an

We're probably not going to slip one day and fall into Christian maturity. Prayer is about developing a relationship with God, not just "believing in God." God is consistent with us. Could we try to learn to be consistent with God?

123

hour…I'll pray after I finish changing the oil in the car…I'll pray tomorrow—at Tara," here are daily prayer exercises from a kindred spirit! They may help you get into the habit of praying. I promise—it's worth the effort.

Why Pray?

Good prayer habits act like an incubator for our relationship with God. If we pray, if we show up, God has a much better chance of getting through to us. Over time, we know ourselves better.

I have great news: prayer affects more than you! Our research demonstrates that when people pray, talk with a prayer partner, and talk about faith with others at church, something exciting happens. Relationships improve. Families tend to get happier. People who pray mysteriously "have the words" when the Holy Spirit arranges situations for them to talk with people who don't have a conscious faith life. Prayer helps us listen to other people for real.

Prayer changes things—within us and for others.

We're probably not going to slip one day and fall into Christian maturity. Prayer is about developing a relationship with God, not just "believing in God." God is consistent with us. Could we try to learn to be consistent with God?

Prayer Partner

Talking about your reaction to these exercises with someone else will maximize the benefit of your prayer. Each "fifth day" in the prayer journal contains suggestions for talking or praying with your prayer partner. Could you be a prayer partner with the person who invited you to do this study? Whatever you decide, please talk about your response to these exercises with at least one other person, once a week, in person or by phone. Budget at least a "check-in" time about everyone's prayer when your *Unbinding Your Soul* study group meets each week. Half the fun is getting to see how everyone's individual prayer is progressing.

Prayers for Can't-Sit-Still <u>and</u> Artistic Types!

Not everyone thinks, works, learns or prays the same way. Some people are highly creative and learn best when they use their hands, voices, and bodies. Do what works for you—do what you love. Draw, act out parts, sculpt a model of the scripture! Some of us pray best while moving or talking. My ADHD (attention deficit hyperactivity disorder) friends have fits when they even ***think*** about sitting in one place in silence. ***Motto: give new ways to pray a chance, but pray in the ways that work for you!*** The prayer journal sections of this book offer you 40 days of varied prayer exercise suggestions. I could never list all the options, but here are a few ways you can tailor them to the way you're wired:

- Walk around the room while you read the scripture, timing the words with your steps or your breath
- Read the scripture out loud
- "Act out" the Bible story

■ DRAW or form a Play-doh™ figure of the scripture

■ Read the scripture sitting, then pray walking. Return to your chair to sketch or write notes.

I include a "Notes, Lists, Drawings, Thoughts, Insights" section for each day. Make a list, sketch a drawing, do whatever makes the day's exercise most effective and memorable to you. Experiment. Have fun with it. If you don't know what you want to do, ask God. You may be surprised at some of the nudges you get from the Spirit!

Same Time, Same Place

William Law, a wise 18th-century English theologian and writer, influenced generations of pastors, including the Wesleys, from whose work the Methodist churches began. Law suggested that we have one special chair in which to pray each day. Choose a (not too) comfortable, straight-backed chair in a room away from family traffic patterns. Only pray and do your devotions in this chair during these weeks—no mystery novels, no TV, no phones, no iPods,™ no directing kids' homework! Keep your supplies right next to your chair so you don't have to interrupt your prayer time to go get something.

Choose a specific time to try to pray each day. Although I have written as if you are praying early in the morning, you may be drawn to a time after breakfast, when everyone else has left the house; lunch time in your office; or evening (instead of TV or before bed). If in doubt, ask God what time you should choose. Don't drive yourself crazy about exact adherence to A Rigid Plan, but consistency will help you develop the habit of prayer! Light a candle each day as you sit down, if you want to. Remind yourself that Christ is right there with you. If a candle feels stupid, don't do it! You can develop simple habits that will help grow your relationship with God.

Prayer, Breathing, & Neurological Stuff

I don't understand this well enough to explain it scientifically, so just trust me on this one. Our bodies pray better when we're sitting up straight (not militarily straight, but don't slump or bow your head). Sitting cross-legged is fine. Somehow it helps to keep your spine straight and your head up.

Some people get cold when they pray for a long time. If you're wired this way, keep a blanket handy or wear a sweater!

Breathing helps us focus. Part of prayer is about slowing down and being aware of God, not our own obsessive thoughts and agendas. A couple of deep breaths help. Imagine that you're letting your tension go out of your body when you exhale. Truly, it's a neurological deal.

So let's have agreement, alright? I'm *not* going to start every prayer exercise day saying, "Light your candle to remind you Christ is right there with you. Breathe in fully. Exhale, and imagine that all of your tension and worries are leaving your body with that big breath. Inhale again. Exhale. Let your face and jaw and body relax." That would be annoying. I want to save words on those pages. I don't want army guys and litigators rolling their eyes. BUT, when I say, "Sit and calm down" at the beginning of a prayer day, that's what I mean! Just try it for a week, okay? If you don't like the candle, forget about it. But keep breathing. And, like I said, keep your spine straight.

Supplies

- Bible
- Pens, pencils, art supplies, clay
- Reading glasses
- *Unbinding Your Soul*
- Prayer candle and matches
- Journal or extra writing paper
- 3 X 5 cards

Plan Ahead

You will need to make a few, simple preparations for the prayer days listed below.

1. **Prayer partner days** are Day 5 of each week. You'll want to look at that day's reading before you arrange to meet with your prayer partner, whether in person or by phone. It may be more convenient to meet on a different day. That's great—just try to do the other days in order.

2. **Extra supply days,** when a household object will help your prayer:

   - *Week B: Day 3:* A backpack, shopping bag with straps, or a big purse; rocks, or bricks, or books or weights—heavy things that will fit in the bag. If you're frail, use socks or something light.

   - *Week B: Day 4:* A newspaper, news magazine, or go to an Internet news source

   - *Week C: Day 5:* Preparation. Read the prayer exercise ahead of time, talk with your partner, and decide where you're going to meet to pray.

   - *Week D: Day 3:* String of pearls, necklace, Mardi Gras beads or prayer beads

Pattern of the Exercises

You will have a scripture, a prayer exercise, note-taking space and a closing prayer for each day of the next six weeks. Some days suggest an exercise to be carried out during the day, but you will always have your scripture and prayer time first. If you do these exercises in the evening, do the prayer at night then the exercise the next day. The weeks' prayers follow a pattern:

Days 1–4: A new prayer exercise

Day 5: An exercise to do with your prayer partner

Day 6: A review/reflection day when you:

> (A) Review this introduction, read the next chapter, and answer two key questions:
>
>> (1) What are the most important things you've learned this week?
>>
>> (2) What are you wondering about?

Day 7: Group day. Take notes or jot down ideas in your journal.

Bible Readings

Each prayer day starts with a scripture. "Scripture" means "something written." In this case I'm referring to a passage from the Christian Bible. The Bible contains two main parts. The first part, the "Old Testament," is sometimes called the "Hebrew Scriptures." They were written in Hebrew *before* Jesus was born. We date our years as starting with Jesus' birth at time point zero and his death in year 33.

The second part of the Christian Bible is called the "New Testament," or the "Greek Scriptures." The short "books" and letters are about Jesus' life, death and resurrection, and about the new churches that began after his resurrection. They were written in Greek between the years 55 and 125 A.D. (anno domini, which means "Year of our Lord"), or C. E. (common era)

You may have studied the Bible for years and feel very comfortable with biblical literature and history. You may not own a Bible. If you don't have a Bible, could you ask a pastor or the person leading your group where to get one and which translation they suggest? I would suggest a study Bible, because they explain things.

I list a scripture for each day by the name of the "book" of the Bible. (These "books" are really sections of the Bible. Some of them are very short. They're often called by the name of the person who wrote it, or in honor of the person whose ideas are collected in that book. The first number after the name of the book is the number of the chapter. Then there's a colon (:). The next number is the number of the verse in the chapter. Most Bibles include a list of the books of the Bible somewhere near the front. The books consist of different types of writings—histories, letters of advice, poetry, writings from prophets and "Gospels," which are four different accounts of Jesus' life. Your Bible may have tabs on the side so you can get to different books quickly.

Don't gut this out alone. Not everyone flips through the Bible to the exact spot in that intimidating way! *Loads* of people have questions about the Bible, and lots of them have been sitting in churches for 30 years. Ask for help *before* you get frustrated or feel awkward! If you aren't sure how to locate the scripture readings, ask your group leader or best friend in the class to mark the next week's passages in your Bible with Post-it[R] notes—no fuss, no muss and no lost time! (Read the notes in your study Bible—they're fascinating.)

P.S. If anyone quotes something you suspect is from the Bible, go to *www.Google.com*. You can find almost any quote there!

Keep the Main Thing the Main Thing!

The point of these prayer exercises is to help you pray with scripture and to move closer to God. If you are drawn into a certain phrase of scripture, if you feel a sense of God's presence one day, stick with it! Our increasing awareness of the presence of God is what matters in our spiritual lives. The exercises are only a tool to help you try new ways of being more receptive to the Spirit. If you and God are drawn into a "side conversation," it's probably the main thing. Stay with God, not the program!

Remember: if you have questions, when something bothers you or makes you crazy, or if you have a wonderful insight—call someone and talk about it! Enjoy this time.

St. Patrick's Breastplate

Prayers come from the heart. They require only a wish, a thought, an image, a whisper to God. Our prayers need to be real, not poetic.

But if you love the power of anointed words, here is a ninth-century Irish prayer. St. Patrick, the patron saint of Ireland, was a well-educated Roman boy, living in England. Irish raiders kidnapped him. He spent his teenage years in Ireland as a slave. After his escape, now in his twenties, he returned to Ireland to try to bring Christianity to the Irish. This is the prayer he is said to have prayed—for protection and for guidance—before he meet with Laoghaire, the Chief King of the Irish, to talk about the new faith. I love this prayer. (All right, I could probably do without the "...Against spells of women, and smiths, and druids" line, but you can't be selective about an historic text. He means witches, so sisters, you don't need to send me sternly worded e-mails. Blacksmiths—you guys are on your own!)

I arise today
Through a mighty strength
the invocation of the Trinity
Through the belief in the threeness
Through the confession of the oneness
Of the Creator of Creation.

I arise today
Through the strength of Christ's birth with his baptism
Through the strength of his crucifixion with his burial
Through the strength of his resurrection with his ascension
Through the strength of his descent for the Judgment Day.

I arise today
Through the strength of the love of Cherubim
In obedience of angels
In the service of archangels
In hope of resurrection to meet with reward,
In prayers of patriarchs
In predictions of prophets
In preaching of apostles
In faith of confessors
In innocence of holy virgins
In deeds of righteous men.

I arise today
Through the strength of heaven:
Light of sun

Radiance of moon
Splendor of fire
Speed of lightning
Swiftness of wind
Depth of sea
Stability of earth
Firmness of rock.

I arise today
Through God's strength to pilot me
God's might to uphold me
God's wisdom to guide me
God's eye to look before me
God's ear to hear me
God's word to speak for me
God's hand to guard me
God's way to lie before me
God's shield to protect me
God's host to save me
From snares of demons
From temptations of vices
From everyone who shall wish me ill
Afar and near
Alone and in multitudes.

I summon today all these powers between me and those evils
Against every cruel merciless power that may oppose my body and soul
Against incantations of false prophets
Against black laws of pagandom
Against false laws of heretics
Against craft of idolatry
Against spells of women and smiths and wizards
Against every knowledge that corrupts one's body and soul.

Christ to shield me today
Against poison, against burning
Against drowning, against wounding
So that there may come to me abundance of reward.

Christ with me, Christ before me
Christ behind me, Christ in me
Christ beneath me, Christ above me
Christ on my right, Christ on my left

Christ when I lie down, Christ when I sit down
Christ when I arise
Christ in the heart of every man who thinks of me
Christ in the mouth of everyone who speaks of me
Christ in every eye that sees me
Christ in every ear that hears me.
I arise today
Through a mighty strength, the invocation of the Trinity
Through belief in the threeness
Through confession of the oneness
Of the Creator of Creation.

From the Book of Armagh, early ninth century, Ireland

Do it again!

Thirty-five people have attended worship in a western farming community church for the last 30 years. They decided to study **Unbinding Your Heart** *in a small group. Small groups usually consist of eight or ten people, but 28 people showed up. All 28 of them went through the book, praying the prayers, discussing the chapters. The same 35 people showed up for worship.*

At the end of the six-week study, someone said, "We haven't talked enough about this. We need to do the prayers more thoroughly. We've paid for these books. We can get more out of them. We can really pray with these journals this time." So all 28 of them went back. They redid the book. They talked about different ideas from the book. They did the exercises and the prayers more thoroughly. New insights emerged. Still 35 people worshipped.

*Halfway through the **third** time through the book, one of the older gentlemen, a pillar of the church, said, "Why don't we each invite two people to worship next Sunday?"*

They did it. Two Sundays AFTER Easter, 80+ people showed up to worship. The group had been reading so much about faith sharing, prayer, evangelism and welcoming people that they were really nice to the visitors.

The church averaged 75 people in worship all summer.

—Church of the Brethren congregation

New & Improved Facilitators' Guide!
We've added major improvements
based on users' feedback.
Please use THIS version, rather than
the Guide in the first printing.

Facilitators' Guide

Contents

See *www.GraceNet.info* for sermons & supporting materials for your "Soul Sabbatical!"

You have said "yes" to serving as a group facilitator. Thank you. *Unbinding Your Soul* is a spiritual adventure—for you and your co-facilitator, as well as your group. It's best if your church begins with the pastor leading all of the facilitators through the book. Be sure to do the prayer journals and the exercises at the ends of the chapters. This is an experience, not just a book study! You facilitators can continue to meet together weekly after you begin co-leading your group. Pray and talk with each other about your questions, concerns, puzzles, challenges, joys. Share the amazing things you're learning. You all are there for each other. Take advantage of this!

If you haven't done the *Unbinding the Gospel/Heart* process in your church, please do. That's the first step. Unless you are a college group, a new church being started mainly by people *not* raised in a church, or an on-fire growing church, *Soul* will function most effectively as a *follow-up* for an all-church *Gospel/Heart* study, or at least as a follow-up to a small group study of *Gospel* (see the first 2 pages of this book). If you want to try *Soul* without the *Gospel/*

"The average age of our congregation is 70 and new members join just often enough to replace those who have passed away. This means that in 30 years our church will have to close its doors. There is a path towards renewal. It will not cost much money, but it will be the hardest thing we have done in our lives. We in the pews need to start sharing what we think in our heads and feel in our hearts about Jesus. It's what Bonheoffer called Costly Discipleship." (Ouote from Presbyterian college youth group leader encouraging his church to begin *Unbinding*.)

133

Heart preliminaries, go ahead, just let me know how it turns out, okay? (Reese@GraceNet.info—be sure to put "Unbinding Your Soul" in the subject line.) Experiments are good. We'll let everyone know the results when we have them!

Scared to facilitate a group? Read what a group of facilitators felt before they started their group (page 113). Then read about what happened in the church several months later (pages 156–158). Feel better? Want detailed lesson plans? Go to *www.GraceNet.info / Download Resources.*

How to Use *Unbinding Your Soul*

Unbinding Your Soul consists of two parts, each of which takes four weeks. Each half of the book contains four short chapters, small group exercises, and a three-week, personal prayer journal for each group member. ***Never ask anyone — even a facilitators' group — for more than a four-week commitment.*** All participants can join or exit the group at the beginning and end of any four-week section. We see that people *want* to continue after they've started, but always make the commitment a short four weeks!

Groups that have studied *Unbinding the Gospel* or *Unbinding Your Heart* are naturals to use *Unbinding Your Soul* as a Next Step.

Facilitators' Group: Part One — The Experiment, Chapters 1–4. Four Group Sessions, Three Weeks of Individual Prayer Journal. The pastor gathers a small group (8–10 members) of church leaders. Choose people who may have the gifts to co-facilitate a group, or to serve as prayer team members later. Study and pray through Part One of *Soul*. Part One deals with key themes of Christian faith and helps everyone talk about what they believe, what they think, what they wonder about. See *www.GraceNet.info/video.aspx* for videos by groups that have studied *Unbinding Your Soul.* What's your commitment?

- ■ ***Read*** one short chapter each week
- ■ ***Pray*** daily, using the individual prayer journal in this book. (Couples: Please ***don't*** share books. Each person needs a ***private*** journal and a place to take notes.)
- ■ ***Talk*** one day weekly with a prayer partner, using a special fifth day exercise
- ■ ***Meet*** weekly with your group, talk about your prayer life and the chapter and do the exercise at the end of the chapter. (No kidding. Do the exercises!)
- ■ ***Maintain confidentiality***
- ■ ***Arrive*** on time and prepared

Did you like it? Those who want to continue, go on to Part Two.

Part Two—Faith & Courage, Chapters 5–8. Four Group Sessions, Three Weeks of Individual Prayer Journal: Go on to Part Two without much break. Perhaps take a week off, but don't lose momentum! Part Two deals with deeper questions of faith and courage, and also with sharing/discussing faith issues with people who aren't part of a Christian community.

You can now become the Facilitators' Group and move into leadership! At the end of Part Two, members of this group, led by the pastor, continue to meet as a facilitators' group. Pairs of you can lead small groups of people from your church. Perhaps these are groups you already lead — a men's group, a youth group, a small group or Sunday School class. Perhaps you'll offer this as an opportunity for people who are not yet members of a small group. Some of you in the leaders' group may be leading a prayer initiative, to pray for the other leaders, the groups, the church, the people the Spirit may be nudging you to invite into these groups.

Pray daily for each group member AND for the people you don't know yet - the friends they'll invite into the group.

We have discovered that it's crucial to continue two elements: (a) the pastor's active involvement to support leaders as they're leading, and (b) prayer support. Don't send people out to lead without support and back-up! **Large churches:** *Start enough facilitators' groups (led by staff members) so that you have pairs of leaders for all of your groups. This may take a year. Rule of thumb for* **all churches:** *Train 20% of your average worship attendance to be leaders!*

Lead church members through Part One (four-week commitment). You have prayed and studied **Unbinding Your Soul** with your group of friends — now share it with others. Invite church friends into groups. See *GraceNet.info / Download Resources* for lesson plans if the questions and exercises at the back of the book don't feel like enough for you. Karl and David Kling, brilliant, Presbyterian pastor-father and finance-wizard-son, have each led many **Unbinding Your Soul** groups. They developed a Leaders' Guide for you! See videos of David and one of the college groups from First Presbyterian Church, Gainesville, Florida at *www.GraceNet.info/video.aspx.* Many experienced leaders will find the exercises at the ends of each chapter perfect for them. If you're a new leader, or the kind of facilitator who loves to see great lesson plans spelled out, you'll be delighted with Karl and David's Leaders' Guide.

Encourage church members to re-covenant to study Part Two, Faith & Courage. Groups typically want to continue. You could add more church members at this point.

We have discovered that it's crucial to continue two elements: (a) the pastor's active involvement to support leaders as they're leading, and (b) prayer support. Don't send people out to lead without support and back-up!

After you've studied *Faith & Courage,* and perhaps a short break, lead those who want to invite friends into The Experiment (Part One) to keep going for the really exciting stuff – conversations with friends who want to try a " no-obligation test drive" of Christianity. Your group could double. Some people may invite two or three people into the group. A few friends may not say yes. Be prepared (with books, prayer candles and in your heads) for more! You may choose to divide the group into two sections that meet on two nights, or you could meet in different rooms in the same house. Eight to ten is always the optimal size for a small group. If your group divides, one leader can move on with each group, and select another member of each new group to serve as co-leader. (See how this helps with leadership development? Each seasoned leader can help a new person step into leadership.) The new leaders join the Leaders' Group. You might take a short breather between the two parts. Just don't lose momentum.

Whom to invite? See the introduction – ask neighbors, family members, new visitors to your church, new members classes. (Some churches ask special mentors to study *Unbinding Your Soul,* then invite brand new church members into a study of Part One, The Experiment. This helps tremendously with integration of new members!) See the introduction (page xi) and the appendix to chapter 7 (page 101) for ideas of whom and how to invite.

A Soul Sabbatical - All-Church Study of Soul
Want to do an all-church study? Many churches that have experienced an "E-vent," an all-congregational study with ***Unbinding Your Heart*** understand the power and excitement that can emerge from a six-week, all church "Sabbath," or "Sabbatical." Whole churches come alive when everyone discusses the same ideas, prays with the same prayer journal, listens to sermons, worships with liturgy and music that pull together what you've been thinking about all week - and carries it to a new level! We suggest that churches cancel all ordinary meetings during this "Soul Sabbatical." (Maybe you want to call it your "Soul Sabbath.") Offer this time to God, to pray, to talk, to be the church for real!

Unbinding Your Soul works beautifully as simply small group material. That was my original idea, but so many of you have asked for resources for an all-church Soul Sabbatical that we're going to help you create one. Dawn Weaks, a great Disciples of Christ preacher, wrote the sermons for the ***Unbinding Your Heart*** E-vent. Dawn is working on sermons for the Soul Sabbatical. They'll be available in the fall of 2010. One of the most powerful music ministers in the country (we'll announce who he is soon) is putting together music and liturgy that will be ready by the spring of 2011. Have you developed children's resources? Send them to us! We'll post the most helpful at *www.GraceNet.info / Download Resources / Exclusive Downloads.* **Password: Unbinding**

If you haven't done an E-vent in your church, get a copy of *Unbinding Your Church: Pastor's & Leaders' Guide* that goes with *Unbinding the Gospel & Unbinding Your Heart.* Use it as your model for doing an all-church study. Watch "What's an E-vent?" at *www.GraceNet.info/video.aspx.*

A Soul Sabbatical needn't be as intense or broad-based as an *Unbinding Your Heart* E-vent, where we urge all churches to get 85%+ of their average worship attendance involved in an *Unbinding Your Heart* small group. The *Unbinding Your Soul* sermons and worship resources will work beautifully even for people who aren't studying *Unbinding Your Soul.* That said, don't be timid! Everyone doesn't need to invite a friend into a SOUL group, but everyone can pray! The more people involved, the more God will be able to use your church. Reach for 100% involvement. *Think* what the Spirit could do with that!

The Soul Sabbatical is in two, three-week parts. The first coincides with the last three weeks of your church groups' Part Two study of Faith & Courage. The second part coordinates with your Experiment groups' last three weeks of Part One (chapters 2-4).

Eight to ten is always the optimal size for a small group. If your group divides, one leader can move on with each group, and select another member of each new group to serve as co-leader. (See how this helps with leadership development? Each seasoned leader can help a new person step into leadership.)

And so on... Keep Going

Unbinding Your Soul is designed so that groups can choose to keep going after the Soul Sabbatical. The new people in The Experiment Groups will probably want to re-covenant for another four weeks to study Part II, Faith & Courage, together. At the end of that, they may feel called by God to invite some of their friends into a group. Just drop and add people at the four-week points. It works. Let this become an organic movement. The Facilitators' Group will keep things organized and you'll learn as you go. After the Soul Sabbatical, use *Unbinding Your Soul* to integrate new members, as a series of four-week studies for your college and high school ministries, as a follow-up to Alpha. Some churches are beginning to see *SOUL* as an on-going small group process that helps the church move beyond the walls of the building, into coffee shops, homes, offices, hearts and families. Your prayer, your patience and your courage will help Christ change lives.

Here are some possible time-tables:

Group Planning Chart

GROUP	CHAPTERS	WEEKS	ASSIGNMENT BEFORE 1ST MEETING	LENTEN SOUL SABBATICAL	FALL SOUL SABBATICAL
1. Facilitators' Group (if at least 2 groups in your church - pastor leads)	1-4 5-8	8 Facilitators' Group continues for leadership discussions & prayer so long as groups meet.	Introduction, Chapter 1, *Using Your Prayer Journal.* Start Week A of prayer journal the day AFTER first group meeting	Spring or if compressed, Sept 15-Nov 15	Spring
2. Church Groups (each led by a pair of facilitators)	1-4 5-8	8	Introduction, Chapter 1, *Using Your Prayer Journal.* Start Week A of prayer journal the day AFTER first group meeting	Part One, Fall (latest Nov 15-Dec 15)	Part One, Pentecost or as late as Sept 15-Oct 15
				Part Two,* between Jan 15th and Ash Wed	Part Two, early fall, or as late as Oct. 15–Nov 15
3. Experiment Groups (church groups + friends. Divide to maintain size at 8-10 members & 2 leaders)	1-4	4	Introduction, Chapter 1, *Using Your Prayer Journal.* Start Week A of prayer journal the day after group meeting	Lent (end before Palm Sunday)	October, or as late as Nov 15-Dec. 15
4. Some Experiment Groups re-covenant to study Faith & Courage	5-8	4	Chapter 5, *Using Your Prayer Journal.* Start Week D of prayer journal the day AFTER first group meeting	Pentecost	Jan-Feb
5. Some continuing Experiment Groups re-covenant to study The Experiment with *new* friends.	1-4	4	Introduction, Chapter 1, *Using Your Prayer Journal.* Start Week A of prayer journal the day after group meeting	Summer or Fall	Lent
Etc....					

---

    * Soul Sabbatical Sermons and worship resources, denoted with gray shading, relate to the Church Groups' last three weeks (the Sundays following week-day study of chapters 6-8), then recommence to follow The Experiment Groups' study of chapters 2-4.

Leading an *Unbinding Your Soul* Group

Many of you are seasoned leaders and teachers. You can use this experiential book with groups that are already formed (Sunday School classes, small groups, membership classes, a ministry team in your church) OR you can gather a group of friends JUST to work through the **Unbinding Your Soul** experience. Here are key elements to success:

- **Co-facilitate the group!** While one person is actively leading, the other can quietly pray for the group. You'll have a friend with whom to share perceptions and ideas. Enjoy using your different strengths as you lead the group and pray for your wonderful group members each day.

- **Small Groups of 8–10, plus leaders.** We have discovered that small groups work best for actual faith sharing.

- **Meet in homes.** The goal of **Unbinding Your Soul** is to help you:

  (a) Deepen your faith, and

  (b) Invite friends who don't have a faith community or a faith background to try a "test drive" of Christianity - an "experiment" in classic Christian spirituality and community

  Many people who don't attend church (your friends!) are more comfortable in homes than in church buildings. Decide based on your situation. It is more important to have the group meet in homes for Part One (the "Experiment Groups") than for Part Two (the "Church Groups.")

- **Home group settings.** If you're meeting in homes, make sure there are no distractions. If you have children, make sure baby-sitting is in place before the meeting starts, and allow follow-up time for discussion! Let the house be quiet—turn off all phones, music and TVs. Make sure the house is clean, that there are pens, pencils, Kleenex, extra Bibles and plenty of comfortable chairs (only two people per couch works best). Coffee, tea and soft drinks are a choice. You might want to have refreshments afterwards, at least for the last meeting of each four-week segment.

- **Pray daily** for each group member AND for the people you don't know yet—the friends they'll invite into the group for The Experiment (Part One).

Ask your church's prayer team to pray for your group. Keep them informed of how the group is going, without divulging confidential information, so that they can focus their prayer for your group.

If you don't have a prayer team, see chapter 5 of **Unbinding Your Church** for suggestions on starting one.

Goal for Facilitators:
You are *not* here to
TEACH. You are here to
help group members
experience the gospel,
prayer and a loving
Christian community.
The less you talk, the
better.

■ *Prayer Partners* will help support each person's intention to pray each day. Developing spiritual disciplines is a new pattern in most people's lives. Having a prayer partner will help your accountability, growth and fun.

■ *Prayer Triads* are very powerful for most groups. I begin using them from the beginning of Part Two, and on the third week of Part One. If it feels right with your group, you could begin the prayer triads on the second week of Part One. We have discovered that continuing prayer triads with groups, church boards and ministry teams is the one, identifiable factor to keep groups going. Continue using prayer triads weekly even after you finish your Unbinding work, if your group chooses to continue.

■ *Prayer team to support this process.* Keep them informed of how the group is going, without divulging confidential information, so that they can focus their prayer for your group.

■ *Facilitate honest discussion and prayer. Don't TEACH content!* Goal for Facilitators: You are <u>not</u> here to TEACH. You are here to help group members <u>experience</u> the gospel, prayer and a loving Christian community. The less you talk, the better. The more group members talk about their thoughts and personal experiences of God and actually pray, the more they'll get out of it!

■ *Leaders in Spiritual Agreement:* We have discovered a wonderful dynamic of leadership (see Prayer Journal, Week E, Day 5). Two people facilitate better together than any one of us could lead alone. While one is leading, the other can watch to see which kinds of leadership work best with your group. The "non-leading" facilitator should also be praying for the group and the co-facilitator. Alternate leadership—agree in advance about who will lead each segment of the group time. Talk about the week's session together ahead of time. Pray for your group members together at least once a week. Pray for each member of your group, each other, and the people they meet each day.

Good Group Dynamics Rules

How do you lead a group? Here are a few suggestions:

Confidentiality & Covenant. Ask your group to commit to rules of group confidentiality at the first meeting. If everyone is willing, it is best if all sign the covenants on page 10 and 67.

Preparation, punctuality & attendance. Groups function best if each member commits to reading the chapter assigned **before** the group meeting each week. During the first session, when you discuss confidentiality, ask that they each do their individual prayer exercises each day. Raise the bar high for preparation, punctuality and attendance! If the group agrees on clear expectations at the beginning of your four weeks, your time together will be happier and more productive.

Fish for answers! Don't tell them! It's much better to ask questions than to state truths. We remember 90% of what we say and only 10% of what we hear! Try to help people express their own developing thoughts and feelings. "What do you think about this?" tends to be more helpful to people than, "The author says…"

Get personal—avoid abstract discussions! The more group time spent doing exercises, talking about personal reactions, how people are doing with the prayer journals and actually praying, the better.

Spend the first 10-15 minutes of each session helping people talk about how their individual prayer life has gone this week. (This is listed as the first discussion question at the end of each chapter.)

Length of sessions. You have free scope here. Some groups love hour-long sessions. You have plenty of material for an hour and a half discussion/experience. The majority of churches discover that sessions of an hour and 15 minutes work best.

Be punctual. Honor the time. Start and end on the minute of the appointed time. Group meetings that drag on and on are one of the major reasons for dissatisfaction with a new group. Keep time precisely on discussion segments suggested for exercises and signal ending times with a gong or bell. Honor the ending time. No matter how fabulous the discussion is at 7:59. End. On time!

Do the exercises. We have discovered that groups that spend about half of their time praying and doing the experiential exercises get the most out of it. Most people will want to do **anything but** the exercises. Push them a little! It's your job, and it will help!

Accountability (covenants, expecting preparation, asking how prayer journals are going, etc.) is a blessing to most people. We have discovered that it statistically increases group effectiveness.

Get Personal – Avoid Abstract Discussions! The more group time spent doing exercises, talking about personal reactions, how people are doing with the prayer journals and actually praying, the better.

Facilitators' Groups Meetings

Here are suggestions for your weekly facilitators' meetings. Use what's helpful to you:

- ■ **Do prayer triads for the first ten minutes.** Use the prayer exercise for triads on page 41.

- ■ **Discuss how your groups are going.** What's working well? What needs to be shifted? How are your members responding to the study? What are your biggest questions or frustrations? What exciting things are happening in your group? How's your prayer for your group going? How are group members changing?

- ■ **Look at next week's material,** worship and events connected with the study. Talk.

  - • Will your group invite your Experiment Friends to church? (See chapter 3, page 41 and *A Note to Pastors*, page 147.) Perhaps your church could hold a prayer vigil at the beginning of your study of Part Two. (See suggestions in ***Unbinding Your Church*** & download model from *www.GraceNet.info / Download Resources / Public Downloads*.) Plan and coordinate details. Be creative!

  - • **Pray together** for each other, your group members, all the people they can help move into a deeper relationship with Christ or with the church, and for the church itself.

Supplies

You'll need three items for each participant. You'll need to order for both the Church Group and The Experiment Group at the same time. Here's how to estimate numbers needed:

1. **Bible** available for ***each*** Experiment Group participant (estimate at same number as original Church Group. Some may have them, but be sure you have a supply available.)

2. **Prayer candles** for each Church Group member (1 for Church Group member, 1 for friend in Experiment Group, plus 10% extras for group candles and extra friends)

3. **2 copies of *Unbinding Your Soul* for each Church Group member** (1 for Church member, 1 for friend, plus 20% extras for friends who don't participate but would like to keep the book and for extra friends. You can get "emergency" shipments most quickly from Chalice Press (www.ChalicePress.com), and you can return unused copies to them.)

Advice from a Facilitator:

"We are opening ourselves to the Holy Spirit. We are taking the lid off our vessels. Laying a foundation. I'm learning as a leader to be persistent. Don't get stuck. Pray and open yourself up."

Order books and candles for both the original Church Groups and The Experiment Group Friends at least a month before your Church Groups start. Be certain that you have study Bibles in whatever translation your church prefers available for all members of the Part One Experiment Group. Some people may not own a Bible, or have only a tiny print King James Version from their grandmother! Ask Church Group (Part Two) participants to make sure the people they invite have a Bible that will work well for them. *The Message*[1] is a wonderful paraphrase of the Bible, but it doesn't designate verses, so it might not work well for the biblical study in *SOUL*.

Candles: I'd suggest a 3" in diameter, 6" or 9" tall, white, wax, unscented pillar candle. You don't want anything that seems fussy or wimpy to guys.

Books: Order two books per Church Group participant+20%, one month before the groups start. You are praying that each person who starts the study will invite a friend into the group. *Therefore, count your original participants and order two copies for each person, with a few extras.* A few people may not invite someone. Some people may invite two or three friends into the new group. Some people you invite may not be able to do the study because of a scheduling conflict, but they may want to keep the book. Several of your groups may continue on, with The Experiment Friends inviting *their* friends into another round of Part One studies. So be certain to order extras. If you order from Chalice Press directly (800.366.3383), you can return unused copies.

Check the web site (www.GraceNet.info / OrderBooks) to see latest supply issues, sales, bulk rates, etc. Updated contact information and web links are on the web site.

*Note: Be sure to order an individual copy of **Unbinding Your Soul** for each participant. Married couples have tried to share **Unbinding** books with prayer journals. We've discovered it doesn't work. Think of these books as being like those little, red, gilt-edged diaries with brass keys that 13-year-old girls hide under the sweaters in their second dresser drawer. This is one time when sharing isn't a good thing!*

A Final Word—Keep the Bar High!

Unbinding the Gospel and *Unbinding Your Heart* small group facilitators have discovered a wonderful dynamic. People like accountability. They like to be part of a process that has appropriate structure and clear demands. We asked three group leaders to tell us something they've learned as they led their groups. Here are their answers:

Facilitator's Discoveries:

"I realized that I can remind people and help them be accountable and they don't think of it as nagging. I also pray each day for my co-leader, for every member of our group and for the people I don't even know yet whom God may be preparing to be in this group. This prayer, and our prayer team's support, is changing the way I lead groups at work, as well as this *Unbinding* Group."

1. *Jim:* "We are opening ourselves to the Holy Spirit. We are taking the lid off our vessels. Laying a foundation. I'm learning as a leader to be persistent. Don't get stuck. Pray and open yourself up."

2. *Akesha:* I realized that I can remind people and help them be accountable and they don't think of it as nagging. I also pray each day for my co-leader, for every member of our group and for the people I don't even know yet whom God may be preparing to be in this group. This prayer, and our prayer team's support, is changing the way I lead groups at work, as well as this *Unbinding* Group.

3. *Stan:* "People seem more willing to accept leadership than I thought. They are more willing than I thought to do intense and hard things. It's a real kick to see people getting excited about this."

This is a high commitment process. People will love it more and get much more out of it if you ask about how their prayer life is going each week. Start on time! Pray for your group each day. This can be a huge adventure, not just another little program with a bunch of checklists!

Have a wonderful time serving your group. Our research discovered many life-long church members, even pastors, who are quite shy about their faith. We certainly don't wear our hearts on our sleeves! Just keep praying and gently urging people to talk openly, share and pray bravely. Wonderful things can unfold. When you're not sure what to do with your group, sit quietly for a moment and pray for everyone. Pray that Christ will speak into your mind any words that would be helpful to say. Be patient. God will work miracles if we are patient, pray and stay as open as we can be to the Spirit's nudges.

More Resources: *www.GraceNet.info*

■ *Download Resources:*

- Detailed lesson plans
- Sermons & resources for your Soul Sabbatical (under Exclusive Downloads, password: Unbinding)
- Prayer Vigil Model
- Interviews (see p. 9)

Sidebar:

This is a high commitment process! People will love it more and get much more out of it if you ask about how their prayer is going each week. Start on time! Pray for your group each day. This can be a huge adventure, not just another little program with a bunch of checklists!

- Church Hospitality Survey
- Mainline Evangelism Project Sociological Report (Wenger & Reese)
- Other churches' sermons, music & invitation suggestions (Send us yours!)

■ *Multimedia:*

- Videos
- Photos

■ *Buy Books*: We'll keep the web site updated for current sales on books, availability, any supplier delays, bulk purchase discounts, etc. Contact us if you have questions or run into any problems of which others should be aware.

■ *New Lilly Endowment Grant:* Contact us to see if you are a good fit for the *Unbinding the Gospel Project*–a new grant to support groups of congregations working with the **Unbinding the Gospel Series** and reports of our lastest research.

> "People seem more willing to accept leadership than I thought. They are more willing than I thought to do intense and hard things. It's a real kick to see people getting excited about this."

> Just keep praying and gently urging people to talk openly, share and pray bravely. Wonderful things can unfold. When you're not sure what to do with your group, sit quietly for a moment and pray for everyone. Pray that Christ will speak into your mind any words that would be helpful to say. Be patient. God will work miracles if we are patient, pray and stay as open as we can be to the Spirit's nudges.

---

[1]Eugene Peterson, *The Message* (Colorado Springs: NavPress, 1995).

When everyone says no…

*The almost-retired pastor of a small church in the Unbinding the Gospel Project told his coach there was no way in the world that his people would do a book study. "They won't read. They don't like new ideas. They just won't do anything different. And they **really** don't like evangelism." The coach helped the pastor sort through options for helping his people get excited about the book. The pastor still ended the call saying, "I just know I'm not going to be able to get anyone to do this."*

The pastor was right. Not one person in that church would read the book or talk about it.

So the pastor prayed, then went to get some lunch.

This is a little town. The place to get lunch if you don't go home is the bar. So the pastor put down his sandwich, fries and Diet 7-Up at a table. He held up a copy of a book with a red ribbon and poke-your-eye-out scissors on the cover and projected his voice clearly across the room, "Hey! I'm going to do a study over here about God, and faith, and having new hope in your life. Does anybody want to talk about this? Come on over."

Five people picked up their beers and baskets of peanuts, moved over and sat down. They talked for an hour and a half.

Six weeks later, thirty of them were meeting for an hour and a half every Saturday afternoon. They read the book, they argued, they talked, they prayed, they laughed.

A few of them started drifting into the church on Sunday morning. The church people were dubious, but polite.

The last I heard, the bar group decided to do "that communion thing" one Saturday afternoon. They got a couple of stale rolls from behind the bar. The pastor didn't want to ask what they'd used for the wine. He'd been on a fishing trip in Canada that week.

CHAPTER 11

Note to Pastors

Thank you for supporting your people through these weeks! Here are my suggestions for what you can do to help this process succeed:

1. ***Serve the Group Facilitators:*** You lead the facilitators. Their meetings form the foundation for the groups' ministries. Spend at least half of your group time praying, talking about your own spiritual growth and life issues. THEN discuss issues that have arisen during the week in their groups. Pray for each of the facilitators' groups each time you're together, both before they're actually formed, and then when they're actually meeting as groups. (Follow suggestions for small groups in the Facilitators' Guide in this book as you lead the Facilitators' Group.)

2. ***Prayer for the Groups:***

   ■ Will you pray daily for your church, the facilitators, current group members, and the friends who could join The Experiment? Your prayers as a pastor are crucial to this process.

   ■ Form an intercessory prayer group to pray for your Experiment Groups—both before they start and as they are meeting each week. (Follow the suggestions for prayer groups in ***Unbinding Your Church,*** the green ribbon book, chapter 5).

3. ***Worship for weeks following chapters 3 and 4 Group Meetings—OR a Soul Sabatical?*** You may choose to use the Soul Sabbatical online resources. If not, think about some special worship when your Experiment Groups (church people and friends) study chapters 3 and 4. The Experiment Groups may

147

decide to attend your worship service together on the Sunday following their study of chapter 3. If the friends like the worship service, they might return the following week.

■ *Please read and preach from scriptures that the groups have used for prayer exercises.* I suggest Isaiah 40:28-31 and Matthew 6:25-34; 1 Peter 5:6-7 for the first week. You could follow this with scriptures from their next week's prayers the following Sunday. (I know this goes against the grain for Common Lectionary preachers, but think how wonderful it could be for someone who has never attended church to hear you preach your sermon on a text they have prayed with and studied!)

■ *Great music!* Could you arrange something special like Jazz, Gospel, great local music (Country-Western in Tennessee, cowboy music in Oklahoma, Irish fiddling in Boston, the kids' choir singing—you know your people!), or modern music that coordinates well with the scriptures?

■ Our research with the most effective evangelistic congregations revealed *three elements of worship that annoy or embarrass* people who have not been inured early to church life:

  ~ Greetings at the beginning of worship that single out visitors or make them feel conspicuous (*__Never__* ask visitors to stand "so we can all see who you are!")

  ~ Passing of the Peace (Sorry about that if you're emotionally or theologically attached to it, but it was a clear finding in visitors and new members in both contemporary and highly liturgical services.)

  ~ Hand-holding during prayers

4. *Lunch after worship:* I suggest that Experiment Groups go out to lunch together right after worship on the Sunday after they discuss chapter 3. (Church members—pick up the tab for your guests.) *The next week* you all might think about having another great worship experience, coordinated with their studies after chapter 4 *and* schedule a barbeque or lunch after worship on that Sunday. *HAVE FUN!*

5. *Misc. suggestions:* I get a lot of e-mail from pastors. I see two recurring glitches that are easy to fix. So here's freebie advice:

■ *Add an automatic signature to the bottom of all of your e-mails.* Include your full name, church name, address, phone number with area code, and web site address. If you don't know how to do this, ask someone to help!

■ *Every church web site needs the church phone number with area code on the home page, a "Contact Us" section, a staff section and lots of pictures of people!*

  ~ New people need to see up-to-date, busy schedules of activities to which they're invited, with descriptions. Please lead with these.

  ~ Please *don't lead* with your church's history or denominational history. Members know it. Visitors often take it as a signal that you're more bound up in your past than in the present (or them). Look at the web sites of big and great churches to see what's possible on a smaller scale for the rest of us.

~ Some pastors leave off staff listings or their own pictures out of misplaced modesty, or some sense of encouraging laity to step up into ministry. This frustrates visitors—they need to see your faces and find contact information quickly.

Help other pastors and church musicians. Let us know what you do for your invitation Sundays. Send sermon manuscripts, music ideas, Sunday School activities for kids, and after-worship lunch and party suggestions to *Soul@GraceNet.info*. Put "Unbinding Your Soul" in the subject line. We'll post some of them on the web site under "Download Resources."

Notes

CHAPTER 12

Next Steps & the *Unbinding the Gospel Series*

You can continue to use **Unbinding Your Soul** in four-week segments as long as it continues organically in your church. Develop new leadership as you go. If you are interested in more, you can do an all-church initiative with the other books of the **Unbinding the Gospel Series**. These books and the process they provide are all grounded in ongoing, major, national research. A current grant, funded by the Lilly Endowment, provides coaching for all-congregational immersion experiences using the first three books of the **Series**.

Research Basis for *Unbinding Your Soul* and the *Unbinding The Gospel Series*[1]

The first research initiative, the *Mainline Evangelism Project* (2002-2007), uncovered dynamics of what makes great churches tick. We discovered that the most exciting, faithful and statistically successful faith communities in the country vary widely in terms of size, setting, theological beliefs, structure, geography, and culture. But three things lie at the heart of all these ministries:

■ People love God. They pray seriously. They live out of a deep understanding that God/Jesus/the Holy Spirit are vivid presences in their lives.

■ Participants in these churches talk about their faith—about what God's doing in their lives, about what they're learning about God. They speak naturally, in everyday language.

■ They care about people outside their own circles of close friends. They talk about their faith during the week.

A new Lilly Endowment study, the *Unbinding the Gospel Project* (2008-), is helping us pioneer ways to help typical churches go from "good to great," in Jim Collins' wonderful words! The process we've developed is working. All-church saturation studies with *Unbinding the Gospel / Unbinding Your Heart* (supported by the leaders' guide, *Unbinding Your Church*) are helping typical people pray, deepen their relationships with Christ, and *want* to share their faith.

Congregations that have worked with the *Unbinding* process thoroughly are taking exciting and effective initial steps toward significant faith sharing. Friends are encountering Christ and moving into powerful, new faith lives. Churches are growing. People have formed into small groups. They want to keep going because they're having so much fun and loving what they're learning.

What's the Barrier? Motivation!

The primary hurdle most congregations face is motivation. People don't *want* to do evangelism. No matter what pastors say or doctrine demands, most Christians have little positive motivation to share their faith. No amount of talking will fix the problem. I see thousands of congregations fail to absorb helpful, time-consuming and expensive coaching, training, consulting, and congregational programs because the programs are all aimed at helping churches do evangelism—they deal with the "HOWs" of evangelism.

You can tell congregations to "be missional" until the cows come home. If they aren't internally motivated to share their faith, they just won't do it. You have to deal with motivation first. THEN you can work on the HOWS. Once we know *why* to share our faith, we'll figure out *how* in organic ways that work.

Unbinding the Gospel (red ribbon), *Unbinding Your Heart* (purple ribbon) and the pastor's & leaders' guide, *Unbinding Your Church* (green ribbon) exist to remedy this problem. Congregations who use *GOSPEL & HEART* well take at least 12–18 months to do an all-church saturation process. *GOSPEL and HEART* help churches start moving.

The first three books in the *Unbinding the Gospel Series* have been in existence for two years. The results of slow, complete saturation of typical churches with this process are exciting, in many cases startling. See *www.GraceNet.info* and download the latest "Report to the Lilly Endowment on the *Unbinding the Gospel Project*" for the most recent discoveries.

All-Church Saturation for Significant Transformation

Think about an all-church saturation experience with *Unbinding the Gospel²* (for the leaders) and *Unbinding Your Heart* (for everyone). Many churches have done a small group study of *Unbinding the Gospel*. We have clear data that show a single study, or studies where groups don't use the prayer journals or the group exercises at the ends of chapters have little transformative effect. What works is a long, slow, saturation process of the entire congregation.

Judicatory pastors: Contact us to discuss forming a group of your congregations to begin working with the **Series** and applying for the *Unbinding the Gospel Project* coaching, substantially underwritten by the Lilly Endowment.

Results of the *Unbinding the Gospel/Heart* Process

The Series is in thousands of congregations at this point. We are in consistent contact with 400–500 churches, so we're getting very clear about what works best in a wide range of churches. We see that you get out of it what you put into it. If you treat **Unbinding the Gospel** and **Unbinding Your Heart** as a book study, they provide a lovely book study. But I have virtually no interest in nice little experiences—I care about actual, systemic transformation. We are seeing that if you work with the **Series** and take it slowly, if the pastor prays seriously (we ask for 30 minutes a day, and it almost kills most of us at the beginning!), if you treat it as an organic pilgrimage with the Spirit, amazing things emerge.

Here are the results we see by the end of a year and a half, in congregations that have taken the process seriously (slowly, pastor praying, following the recommended process, following the Spirit organically):

- Almost all participants say that they are praying significantly more

- Almost all participants say that they feel closer to other people in the church

- Almost all participants say that they feel closer to Jesus

- Most participants report a significant increase in talking about faith issues with people outside their congregation and inviting friends to church

- Increase in worship attendance

- Increase in invitations, numbers of visitors, baptisms

- Small groups established & want to continue

- Church boards/ministry teams operate with greater sensitivity to the Spirit

- Lessened conflict, more congregational excitement and focus

- Ability to navigate difficulties with unity and calm (this recession has shown us a lot about this!)

- Creative new ministries emerge from the laity

- More than half of the pastors report greater joy & energy in ministry

- The process works well in many interim situations

- Greater involvement in ministry to the community, including communities with vastly different demographics than the existing congregations

- Healthy congregations describe the process drawing forth more active leadership—from about 20% of the worship attendance to an additional 40-50% of people into active participation and leadership.

See the first two pages at the beginning of this book for HOW to use the ***Unbinding the Gospel Series.*** For more information, see *www.GraceNet.info* and contact us if you have any questions, or would like to think about pulling together a small group of churches to participate in the *Unbinding the Gospel Project.*

Tested steps for using the *Unbinding the Gospel/Heart* process in your congregation:

1. Pastors—read ***Unbinding the Gospel.*** Do you like it? Does it feel as if it will be a fit for your people? If you're not sure, ask a key lay leader to read it and meet you for lunch in two weeks to discuss it.

> Martha Grace Reese may be available for a phone
> conference consultation with groups of pastors.
> To participate in a call, each pastor
> must have read **GOSPEL**!
> Contact us through *www.GraceNet.info* to discuss a call.

2. ***DON'T* read *Unbinding the Gospel, get all inspired and preach a sermon or do a newsletter article about it.*** That:
   A. doesn't help
   B. creates resistance
   C. scares the horses.
   Preaching won't help. A newsletter article won't inspire. Be quiet. Operate by stealth. Let the group process and the Spirit start working with people. You're trying to help a lay movement emerge.

3. Read the Introduction, chapter 1 and chapter 4 of ***Unbinding Your Church***

4. Start a small group (8–10 people plus leaders) of your quickest adapters to do a test study of ***Unbinding the Gospel.*** Ask the key leaders you think will like it best. (Order one copy per person—they contain individual prayer journals.)

5. Do the study for 8 weeks in a row (don't try it with your once-a-month church board. We're seeing that these studies are interesting, but result in disappointing statistical outcomes. This experiential process needs the intensity of weekly sessions.
   A. Combine chapters 1 & 2, then spend a week each on chapters 3 through 8, combine chapters 9 & 10.
   B. Begin the prayer journals at the back of **GOSPEL** the day after you discuss chapter 3.

6. After the test study, read chapter 2 of ***Unbinding Your Church.*** Discuss with the group whether **GOSPEL** has been helpful with your people. If so, you could keep going.

> Martha Grace Reese is available to help with your
> evaluation with another conference call with your group of pastors.
> If you are invited to form a coaching group (with church board approval),
> formal coaching would begin at this point.

7. Next steps are to do small group studies of **Unbinding the Gospel** with all of your functional leadership—at least 20% of your average worship attendance (include youth group leaders and teachers of all Sunday School classes and existing small groups).

8. If your 20% wants to keep going (keep giving them choice points!), you're ready to plan a six-week, all-church saturation study of **Unbinding Your Heart,** the "E-vent." Use **Unbinding Your Church,** and resources on ***www.GraceNet.info.***

9. We are seeing that congregations that do the E-vent on their own average 40–50% participation in the E-vent. Congregations participating in the *Unbinding the Gospel Project* average 85% of worship attendance in 6-week, small group studies.

10. The greater the percentage of a congregation that studies **Unbinding Your Heart,** the greater the chance of significant congregational transformation.

11. Steps 1-10 can take 12-18 months. This process is organic. It requires a long runway. Don't rush it, but keep it thorough and don't lose momentum.

12. A few congregations do a beautiful job doing the full E-vent process using **Unbinding Your Church: Pastor's and Leaders' Guide** on their own, but we see almost double the markers of actual personal and congregational transformation in churches that take advantage of the Lilly-funded coaching process.

Note: We see statistically significant, transformational changes in congregations in which at least 85% of their average worship attendance participates in a small group study of **Unbinding Your Heart**. The church in story 4 in (pages 95–97) of **Unbinding Your Soul** holds the current world record for the percentage of people to participate in small groups! The church had declined in worship attendance from 275 to 110 over a 35-year period. The co-pastors are wonderful. They had served the church for five years, won trust, and they pray. They pray seriously. They took this process very slowly, methodically, and with room for the Spirit. They began with 110 people in worship, and 159 people participated in small groups. Average worship attendance for the same 3-month period a year later is 160. Eleven adults were baptized in the first six months of this year. Remember, 145% of their average worship attendance participated in small groups. The congregation grew 46% in average worship attendance over the previous year, and 92 children (and 56 church members) participated in Vacation Bible School. This is the pattern we're seeing. Roughly speaking, the higher the percentage of people who prayerfully study **Unbinding Your Heart** in small groups for six weeks, the greater the impact on the congregation.

Stories and quotations in *Unbinding Your Soul* come from congregations of all sizes from across the country. I've quoted many small church stories. Here's an account from the largest United Methodist church in Illinois.[3]

An Unbinding Focus

Roger Ross, Pastor • First United Methodist Church • Springfield, Illinois

After many years, *Polaroid* finally stopped making their "instant picture" cameras. I loved those things. Decades before the digital age, I remember my Uncle Carl showing off this cutting edge technology that allowed him to take a picture, print it on the spot, and watch it develop in real time. At first, the picture was blank. But after a while fuzzy outlines emerged, and then colors appeared. Finally the whole picture came into focus. The process seemed magical, and it brought delight to young and old alike.

When I first arrived at the church I serve now, we needed a clear picture. Our ministry had gotten a little fuzzy after 187 years in the community. So we conducted a comprehensive survey and discovered what many people already knew. While we had significant strengths, our weakest link was our ability to share our faith with others. Our long-term attendance figures bore that out. Reluctantly, we faced a hard reality: our "don't ask, don't tell" evangelism program wasn't working.

At the same time, Mike Crawford, our Conference Coordinator of Congregational Development, shared with me a series of books by Martha Grace Reese called *Unbinding the Gospel.* Reese, a pastor and former corporate attorney, directed the only major, national study of effective evangelism in mainline churches. She discovered the most pressing need in most mainline churches was to help people discover the joy of prayer and faith sharing.

Reading through the first couple of chapters, I felt it was as if Reese had been to our church. So we connected the dots and began an experiment. We decided to take our staff and the leadership of our congregation through a study of *Unbinding the Gospel* in the fall. If that went well, we would hold an all-church study of the same material in the spring during Lent.

The study in the fall was surprisingly eye-opening and life-changing for our staff and leaders, so we knew it had the potential to transform our congregation. That first group launched us on a prayer and small group journey for almost a year. The staff and teams from our church prayed and fasted, organized and studied the books. They cast vision and helped the rest of the congregation get excited about being a part of a small group during Lent.

To receive the full benefit of the experience, we asked people to do four things: (1) buy a book and read it—a chapter a week for the six weeks of Lent, (2) engage in the daily prayer exercises in the back of the book, (3) join a class or a small group during the study, and (4) commit to attending worship each week.

During Lent, the weekend worship services were tied directly to what the small groups and classes were discussing that week. We intentionally designed the worship experiences to set the stage for the study, including a testimony from someone in the congregation each week.

Finally, after all the prayer, planning and organizational work, God showed up in ways we had never seen before. Over half of our adult worship attendance got involved in a small group and discussed Reese's book, week by week. For 40 days, hundreds of people participated in prayer exercises that wooed us to communicate with God in fresh ways. Many people read scriptures on a daily basis for the first time in their lives and experienced what it was like to do life with a few others in a small group or class. There were direct answers to prayer, new spiritual bonds created, and vivid, personal experiences of the presence of God that brought healing and hope. It really was transformative. To top it off, we found ourselves sharing these experiences with others. We really didn't plan to say anything. It just bubbled out of us. We became evangelists—through the back door.

At a celebration dinner held for the leaders 10 days after Easter, I asked everyone to focus for a couple of minutes on the one experience that spoke to them the most. Perhaps it was a new truth they discovered or a prayer that was answered unexpectedly. It may have been a personal message from God or something that happened in their group. When I reflected for a moment, I knew immediately what captured my heart. That moment came to me on Easter morning.

There was electric excitement in the air as people kept pouring in for Easter. Although we had a full house all morning, it was standing room only at 9:45. We brought in every chair we could find and prayed the fire marshal went to the Baptist Church that day. Things went as expected in the services until it came to the invitation. At each service I asked everyone to remain in an attitude of prayer and invited those who had prayed to receive Christ to lift their heads and look at me. I wanted to pray for them individually. Each time I was overwhelmed by the number of people who looked up. I thought, "Did you understand the instructions?" But the look on their faces told me they did. I began praying for them one by one and then realized there was not enough time. I had to resort to praying for sections. "God bless you in the balcony on the right. Let the seal of the Holy Spirit be upon you in the middle at the back."

In 25 years of ministry, I have never had that happen to me. The Spirit of God was palpable. I just wish I had had a better sermon that day. It was clear they were not responding to what I said. They were responding to the prayer and fasting that many people had been offering for months. They were responding to their friend or family member, their schoolmate or co-worker, who shared some God story in a casual conversation.

I have heard a lot of colleagues wonder if focusing on evangelism and prayer doesn't draw attention away from social action and truly serving others. That's not what Reese discovered in the evangelism study. It's not what happened in our congregation either. When we focused on evangelism, the Spirit opened us to the things of God in all ways. We improved our conscious contact with God through prayer. We invited friends to worship resulting in 30 percent more people attending Easter services than last year. Members and friends prayed to receive Christ into their lives. On Easter we received a special offering to build a much-needed high school addition to the John Wesley School in Liberia. Our sisters and brothers in that West African country needed to raise a huge amount in one offering. Many people thought we would not receive that amount. They were right. We raised $13,000 more than necessary to build the addition. In the long history of this congregation, we have never had that "problem." I also announced during Lent that I felt led to run the Chicago Marathon (my first) as a way to raise support for the people of Liberia. When I asked the congregation to run it with me, I thought maybe 2 or 3 might bite. We now have 42 people training to run the Chicago Marathon in October as a fund-raiser to lift up our friends in Liberia.

It sounds so simple, but miraculous things happen when we pray and share our experiences with God. To the outside observer, it is almost magical. But it is happening in churches all over the country that are choosing to "unbind" the Gospel. Imagine what a picture of new life could look like in your church. Then ask God to bring it into focus.

"See, I am doing a new thing! Now it springs up; do you not perceive it?"
Isaiah 43:19, NIV

---

[1]The **Unbinding the Gospel Series** is a collective title for the "*Unbinding Books*," written by Martha Grace Reese. Currently the **Series** consists of the cornerstone book, **Unbinding the Gospel,** which is designed for small group study by church leaders (20% of worship attendance). Two more books help congregations move the ideas and practices of **Unbinding the Gospel** to the whole congregation, in an all-church study (an "E-vent") of the six-week version of **Unbinding the Gospel,** called **Unbinding Your Heart: 40 Days of Prayer & Faith Sharing** (Chalice Press, 2008). A third book, **Unbinding Your Church: Pastor's and Leaders' Guide** provides guidance through the process, as well as sermons, children's resources, music plans, prayer, planning and activity suggestions. **Unbinding Your Soul** is the fourth book in the **Series,** designed as a follow-up for small groups who have participated in an E-vent. Some congregations may choose to use this book as an introduction to the **Series**. If you try that, let us know how it works (*Soul@GraceNet.info,* put "Unbinding Your Soul" in the subject line).
[2]Martha Grace Reese, **Unbinding the Gospel,** 2nd ed. (St. Louis: Chalice Press, 2008).
[3]Reprinted with permission from *The Current, News of the Great Rivers Conference of The United Methodist Church,* June 2009.

Notes

Notes